THE
TRANSITIONING
MILITARY
LOGISTICIAN

THE TRANSITIONING MILITARY SERIES

THE
TRANSITIONING
MILITARY
LOGISTICIAN

LTC Jay Hicks, Ret, PMP
Sandy Cobb, PfMP, PgMP, PMP

GR8TRANSITIONS4U, INC.

Published by GR8TRANSITIONS4U
GR8TRANSITIONS4U (USA) Inc.
PO Box 13504
Tampa, Florida 33681

USA
Copyright © 2015, Jay Hicks, Sandy Cobb

Hicks, Jay
Cobb, Sandy
The Transitioning Military Logistician
Includes End Notes
ISBN 978-0-9864376-3-2

Printed in the United States of America
Book design by Tamara Parsons
Kensington Type & Graphics

*Dedicated to the Soldiers,
Sailors, Airmen and Marines
of the United States Military.*

Table of Contents

FOREWORD

Every logistician considering or soon transitioning from military service needs to read *"The Transitioning Military Logistician"* and add it to their personal professional library.

A few years ago, while preparing for my own transition from the military I attended a number of preparation programs, including the Department of Defense's - Transition Assistance Program (TAP) and the U.S. Army's - Army Career and Alumni Program (ACAP). When I completed these courses, I left with better interview skills and the ability to put together a resume. However, I felt something was missing. Did I have an accurate translation of my military knowledge, skills, and experiences in my resume? Had I developed a viable employment plan that was inclusive of being hired and advancing within an organization? Did I know what I wanted to do and where to start looking? Literature from various fraternal organizations helped fill some of the gaps, explaining veterans' benefits or financial planning; but little on continuing career development. Something was still missing.

Along comes *"The Transitioning Military Series"* with its second book, *"The Transitioning Military Logistician"*. Will my questions be answered? The innovative approach which this series takes by dedicating a book for each career field targeted is extremely helpful. The format of *"The Transitioning Military Logistician"* flows logically and is easy to follow. A wide variety of career specific subjects are covered. I found the personal assessments in **Chapter 2, Know Yourself** and the discussion on professional certifications in **Chapter 3, Commercial Logistics Basics** to be very valuable in gauging pre-transition preparedness. The information, techniques, and strategies presented are well researched, up-to-date and derived from exemplary resources. Best of all, everything is tailored to military logisticians! It fills in the gaps I was looking for previously. My questions have been answered.

In 1997, while working as the Senior Supply Systems Technician in the Corps Materiel Management Center at Fort Hood, Texas, I first met future author, Jay Hicks. I coached the young Major Hicks on Logistics Functions and Logistics Automation. In turn, he mentored me on Information and Network Technology while introducing more and more commercial terminology in our discussions. He would explain to me and our soldiers that the skills we were developing would transfer to the commercial sector. We needed to know how to assist describing these skills to future potential employers in terms the employer would understand. Jay's insight and genuine concern for his soldiers and their life beyond the military was clearly evident. This concern has grown into a passion today as he continues to assist service members in their military transition to the civilian workforce; an admirable quality that is shared by this book's co-author Sandy Cobb. Together, their mentorship leaps from the pages of this book as they teach and coach us through the transition process.

Transitioning from the military can be overwhelming. *"The Transitioning Military Logistician"* gives you the tools, strategies, and confidence that will guide you through a less stressful and a more successful transition.

CW5 Wade H. Lovorn III, Retired
12th Regimental Chief Warrant Officer
U.S. Army, Quartermaster Corps

CONGRATULATIONS! If you have picked up this book, you are probably ready to embark on your military transition. You may be unaware of the significant logistical experience that you have gained from the military. This book will assist with military transitional challenges and provide some good common sense guidance as you deal with the uncertainties and the associated ambiguities along your journey. By reading and using the tactics in this book you gain a professional advantage, setting into motion a course of action that will reduce transitional stress and create a satisfying and financially lucrative outcome.

Millions of service members have transitioned – now it is your turn. This book, along with its companion guide, will organize the chaos associated with transition, ease your concerns and increase your confidence. Download your free companion guide from GR8MilitaryLog.com. The guide contains copies of reusable assessments, charting forms, a personal strategic roadmap, in addition to process details and examples for using the forms. Keep the companion guide nearby and use it when performing the personal assessments and charting your strategic roadmap.

Leverage your military experience.

Good luck in your transition!

THE TRANSITIONING
MILITARY LOGISTICIAN

Introduction

MILITARY SERVICE IS OFTEN THE CATALYST THAT ALLOWS ORDINARY YOUNG MEN AND WOMEN TO BREAK FREE OF A CHALLENGING EARLY LIFE AND BECOME AN EXTRAORDINARY LEADER. SFC Ronald Saxton, USA, Ret, is one such man. Raised by a single parent in the tough part of Kansas City, Ron enlisted in the military in 1981 as an US Army Automated Logistics Specialist.

Ron retired from the military in 1999 and continued to support the war effort as a contractor working with logistics soldiers in Kuwait. With over two decades of logistics automation experience, Ron soon identified a critical shortcoming in our wartime logistical supply chain. Soldiers engaging the enemy needed critical repair parts to keep the equipment rolling and continue the war's forward momentum. Ron was acutely aware of the logistics automation challenges associated with various automated supply requisition systems within Iraq and Kuwait. He knew there were multiple underlying issues associated with each of the individual systems and the challenges these problems presented for the soldiers and the Army.

> *"I've always felt that I was destined for some great achievement, what I don't know."*
>
> Gen. George S. Patton, USA

Without sustained training for the soldiers, newly fielded and rapidly integrated logistics systems became an increasing challenge for the Army in the Middle East. Knowing he had the knowledge and capability to assist with this challenging issue, Ron rapidly executed an extraordinary plan. He quickly formed a company and won his first government contract providing SARSS training through the Reception, Staging, Onward Movement and Integration (RSO&I) program for young soldiers arriving in Kuwait. This training solution proved invaluable for supporting combat operations in Iraq and Afghanistan and smoothed repair parts flow in theater. Eleven years later, in the private sector, Ron's logistic company continues to expand and last year grossed nearly $9 Million in revenue.

Ron attributes his success to his military training and the discipline he developed while serving as a non-commissioned officer (NCO) in the Quartermaster Corps. He learned to think beyond himself and understand the value of people. Ron believes in teamwork and knows he could not have been a success without understanding people, their needs and how they are the enablers to success. He saw himself as a leader, organizer, innovator and entrepreneur. Ron's military training enabled him to exceed his dreams, while achieving a level of success he could not have imagined as a child growing up inside Kansas City.

Today his company is a premier minority owned small business in the Atlanta area, providing DoD logistical support to the services and employment for over 100 employees and their families. An amazing 70 percent are military veterans!

Change

Nothing is constant, except change. Ron used his knowledge and experience to embrace change. By doing so, Ron created an opportunity for himself and simultaneously helped others while shaping his life and career. You now face changing occupations and potentially your career field. Just like Ron, focus on what you want and what related experience you bring to the table. Knowledge is power. Treat this knowledge as stored-up energy. Move onward to your next career with this knowledge in hand.

How will you handle change? Are you going to be frustrated or are you going to excel? The world will continue to evolve. Are you ready to drive change or will you follow it? By reading this book you are taking charge as you transition to your next career.

In today's work environment, modern workers must be flexible, able to embrace change and reinvent themselves every few years to remain viable. The good news is that you have spent years learning to adapt to ever changing environments while in the military. Your military experience instilled within you the ability to adjust as events occurred. You overcame the challenges of the tumultuous environment you have experienced with the military. This flexibility prepared you for the transformation of your talents. Consider commercial logistics as an exciting challenge for which you are well equipped!

Why Logistics?

As you prepare to depart the service, your future career path could very well be a logistics professional in the commercial or public sector. You may have received expert training from the military that is well suited for the career field of commercial logistics. Logistics specialist, supply sergeant, fuels specialist, load master, medical supply NCO, and hydraulic systems mechanic are just some of the many occupational backgrounds that you developed while serving our country.

Many military non-logistical occupations require logistics skills and responsibility. Even as an infantryman or medical specialist without formal logistics training, you may have supervised and performed logistics functions at various times during your career. Regardless of your military career field, you have learned something about military logistics. You probably ordered, stocked and issued repair parts, clothing and general supplies utilizing the supply system. You've possibly been responsible for transaction follow up and receipt procedures, how to enhance a storeroom layout and storage, and the proper operation of the Government Purchase Card Program. You likely have driven countless miles, performed duties associated with hazardous material control and management or maintained inventory databases for material stocked in warehouses and shipboard storerooms. You may have had On-the-Job Training (OJT) on how to maintain financial records and accounting systems. All of these are examples of the variety and expansive world of logistics, even if you were in a non-logistical career field. If you find these functions interesting and desire to pursue logistics as a potential post military career, then keep reading and learn how your skills may apply.

Logistics is a growing industry in the commercial world. Companies continue to send manufacturing overseas while outsourcing production, consistently providing rewards for logistics providers. Logistics is key to moving this overseas production into and around our country. Globalization continues to push companies to streamline their logistics process to remain competitive. One of the windfalls within the logistics industry is the continued training of logistics workers. Continuing education, certifications and OJT are great enablers. A recent online publication in Figure 1.1 below depicts the top ten reasons

10 REASONS TO CONSIDER A CAREER IN LOGISTICS

- It's A Growing Industry
- Opportunities For All Education Levels
- Variety Keeps It Interesting
- Opportunities For Advancement
- It Doesn't Really Matter Where You Live
- Women Are Stepping Up
- Get Trained By The Government
- Gain International Experience
- Broad Business Disciplines
- Work With Great People

Figure 1.1 | 10 Reasons to Consider a Career in Logistics

to consider a career in logistics.[1] Some of these are elaborated in the next few paragraphs.

Training by the Government

Industry recognizes our military as one of the largest trainers of employees in the logistics field. Many service members come out of the military with great hands-on logistics experience. For example, recent military initiatives include allowing military trained truck drivers to also receive their Commercial Driver's

License (CDL). A movement control specialist can now receive a certification in freight forwarding once they have finished their training.

Interesting Variety

Also making life more interesting, commercial logistics workers receive exposure to a wide variety of occupations. Some of these commercial occupations include aerial port clearance, dispatching, freight forwarding, materials management, inventory control, facility management, procurement, and transportation. This variety, coupled with your talent and versatility, makes logistics a desirable, challenging and interesting career field.

World Wide Work

No matter where you settle after the service, there is a good chance logistics functions are being performed by a commercial company nearby. If you like the global or international flavor, there are plenty of logistics opportunities overseas.

According to the Bureau of Labor Statistics, the median pay for logisticians with a bachelor's degree is $72,780 per year. Further, the job outlook from now until 2025 will grow 22%, far better than the national outlook average.[2] As you mature into the career field of commercial logistics, it will not only offer great pay, but also offer a tremendous growth potential over the next few years. The outlook is indeed optimistic and logistics should offer unfettered growth well beyond this timeframe. Interestingly, there are as many logistic career fields in the commercial sector as in the military. You may not fully understand the civilian terminology and methodologies, but you will be highly successful once you grasp these concepts and see how your military experience has prepared you for them.

> **"The line between disorder and order lies in logistics..."**
>
> Sun Tzu 孫子
> *The Art of War*

Making the Jump

Are you able to translate these skills to the civilian market place? Translating your skill sets and repackaging your resume so that hiring managers can quickly understand your capabilities is imperative. Can you "talk the talk" with a recruiter?

5

Reading this book will give you the confidence to submit a resume knowing you have the right stuff necessary to get the desired commercial position. Gaining an understanding of these nuances between the military and commercial sectors offers insight on transferring and exploiting your skills as you transition to other organizations. Knowing how to construct your resume to show your experience and value is critical to getting noticed and through the interview door.

Transition Strategy

As a military service member, you know the benefit of good planning. You've done it; and it is time to do it once more and plan your own transition. The ability to plan and execute a personal strategy is potentially your greatest attribute. Strategy sets your direction and establishes your priorities in terms of goals. It defines your view of success and prioritizes activities that will make this view a reality. Strategy helps you know what you should work on and what should be worked first. Once goals are set, tactics are used to achieve these goals. While transitioning from the military, start framing your approach by reflecting on questions like:

- *How do I chart a course of action allowing me to unleash my valuable capabilities as quickly as possible after transitioning from the military?*
- *Do I know my best qualities to exploit for my next career?*
- *Do I know what career is best suited for me?*
- *How do I get from where I am to where I want to be?*

This book assists in answering these types of questions, offering guidance during your career change by establishing obtainable goals and objectives. This strategy as outlined in this book is referred to as the "Personal Strategic Roadmap". Interestingly, this process is quite a natural fit for the military mind and the logistical professional.

Why this Book is for You

In the midst of your transition, like the fog of war, you feel unbalanced and confused. It is easy to get lost and realize years later that you have chosen an undesirable path. It becomes painfully obvious if you have not connected all of the dots correctly. The only way to ensure a successful transition is to understand and apply the basics. Careful planning and execution are critical. Just like a military mission, plan well and execute brilliantly. Therefore, understanding your skills in relation to a potential career in commercial logistics is vital. This book and associated website provide assistance in understanding how to perform logistics in a commercial setting and in building your transition roadmap. Practical advice on how to take

> *"Strategy without tactics is the slowest route to victory. Tactics without strategy is the noise before defeat."*
>
> **Sun Tzu** 孫子
> *The Art of War*

the skill sets you have already obtained in the military and applying them to your next career increases your confidence and helps you to become a skilled and trusted logistician. If your transition has already begun, this book may provide answers to critical information you may have missed.

The Value of this Book

Most transition programs offer general guidance by means of generically creating a resume, interview tips, and similar features. You become acutely aware of the transition challenge when you discover the uncertainties associated with career path decisions. It can take years to decide on a path if you do not have an understanding of who you are, what qualities and capabilities you offer, what you desire from life and where you aspire to live.

This book is uniquely suited to help you answer those questions and guide you to the best-suited career path for you and your family. The quality information and assessment tools in this book help you evaluate your current situation and enable you to develop a personal strategic roadmap for your successful transition. A series of personal inventory questions are provided in the areas of environment, characteristics, timing, skills, and desired market place. The assessments assist in the development of your strategic roadmap and guide you toward a potential career path in a marketable area that you and your family will find satisfying and rewarding. Further, this roadmap provides invaluable insight into your motivations, skillsets and willingness to seek out the wide variety of opportunities in your next career as a commercial logistician. The tools in this book help you understand your strengths and weaknesses while increasing your professional skills and making yourself more marketable.

Conventions used in this Book

Each chapter highlights common challenges and provides additional resources for your personal growth. Throughout the book, the Star Box (shown on the right) is used to call your attention to important facts to further investigate and use for transition. Sources vary from websites, book references, credentialing materials, or other programs and resources in the area of military or civilian logistics and logistics management.

Know Yourself *(Chapter 2)*

Chapter 2 discusses the common challenges you may face during your transition. After thought provoking reviews of attributes and skills common to many in the military, you will gain an understanding of the importance of your logistical skills and how they map to the military logistics career fields (Figure 1.2). This mapping will play in an important role in Chapter 3, as we continue to map your skills to civilian logistical occupations.

Great information here.

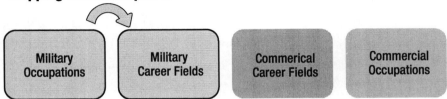

Figure 1.2 | Chapter 2 Mapping - Military Occupations to Career Fields

Additionally, you will explore transition timing, lifestyle desires, and personal tolerance for risk. Multiple assessments covering personal and environmental desires are provided. Through these self-assessments you will gain a documented understanding of your desires as they relate to your transition. Spousal participation in this chapter is recommended. Just like your previous assignments, any transition should be a team decision.

Commercial Logistics Basics *(Chapter 3)*

You have already performed many forms of military supply, maintenance and transportation tasks, just not commercially. In this chapter, you gain an understanding of the complexities of commercial logistics and the vernacular needed to assist your transition and better position yourself for a career in logistics. Using the decomposition of your military skills initiated in Chapter 2, you will be introduced to the military logistic career field alignment to various commercial logistics functions. The commercial sectors are further elaborated into logistic careers, creating the final step to connect-the-dots between military experience and commercial jobs (Figure 1.3). This innovative and unique approach offered in *The Transitioning Military Series* provides a standardized and no-nonsense approach to translate your military skills into viable, realistic and sensible career opportunities.

Mapping Within Chapter 3

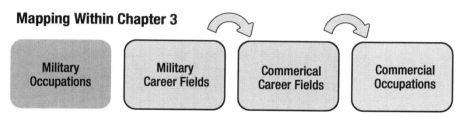

Figure 1.3 | Chapter 3 Mapping - Military to Commercial Career Fields and Occupations

Additionally, you will gain an insider's perspective on career paths, sample job descriptions and corresponding roles/duties. For those wanting to gain that extra edge in seeking a career in logistics management, we explore different educational degrees and certifications you can pursue, focusing on applicability and return on investment. A cross-walk of terminology, resources and the basics of commercial logistics help you to frame your expectations. Through the skills assessment, your answers give you a realistic view of your potential alignment to the various logistics career fields.

The Market Place *(Chapter 4)*

Here we look at three markets for professional logisticians after the service: DoD contracting, civil service and commercial (or corporate) environments. Obviously, there are significant differences between the military and civilian markets. We present many of the different characteristics of the market, outlining pros and cons of each. Entrepreneurship is discussed briefly. The marketplace assessment helps guide you through a process to assist you in determining your risk tolerance, job creativity, income needs, and stress levels.

The Right Fit *(Chapter 5)*

In this chapter you look at your assessment results which are organized and analyzed developing a personal index, unfolding your personal roadmap, and plotting out your best-suited transition. Key indicators from your environmental, characteristics, skills, timing, and marketplace assessments become clearly stated tactics supporting your roadmap. With this information and tactics in hand, you are given options to pursue for your strategic goals and objectives. Executing your Personal Strategic Roadmap will be key to finding and pursuing the best transition path and job based on your assessment results.

Appendices, Website and the Companion Guide

The ultimate goal of this book is to help you assess and organize key facets of your life and experiences to point you towards the best, most lucrative and rewarding career in logistics and logistics management you can achieve. This book and the website provide a repository of easily accessible resources and personal stories to assist you in your transition. Tools, assessments and templates are available in the appendices. Having purchased this book, you are also eligible for the Companion Guide, where reusable tools and templates are provided in electronic format online through the GR8MilitaryLog.com website. Beyond the confines of these pages, the website offers constant updates to materials, statistics, and success stories. These are provided so you can capture and harness the value of this book and its material now and in the future.

Regardless of the path you choose, use this book and the associated assessment tools from each chapter as a system, to assist the development of your Personal Strategic Roadmap, guiding you toward an effective transition.

Companion Guide
Free at
Gr8MilitaryLog.com

The only question remaining is: Have you thought of everything you need to make the right decision? Let's find out!

Many great stories come from every day people, which often inspire and motivate. SFC(R) Ron Saxton with one such story. He stated his success in the government contracting field is directly attributable to lessons learned through a successful 20 year career as an Army logistician.

SFC Ronald Saxton, USA, Ret
Working for the Greater Good

RON SAXTON GREW UP IN A TOUGH ENVIRONMENT. The streets of Kansas City were unkind, and with little encouragement from family, Ron knew he wanted something better. Ron joined the Army Quartermaster Corps, after a brief stint in the Army Signal Corps. He believed the service and the Quartermaster Corps would be enablers, allowing him to achieve great things. After Basic Training (BT) and Advanced Individual Training (AIT), Ron found himself in Germany learning the basics of logistics automation from the inside of a 5,000 line warehouse. Besides learning all about automation and logistics supply flow, Ron found logistics to be a team effort; where a web of people and systems move materials from the manufacturer to the solider in combat. His belief in teamwork and serving a greater purpose permeates all he does today. When Ron retired from Fort Campbell in 1999, he had tremendous aspirations of serving the country using his military logistics skills to provide for his family. Always the patriot, Ron found himself working for Lockheed Martin as a logistics automation project manager for the Army in Kuwait. Three years later, he started a logistics and IT company based in Tyrone, Georgia. Today, after pursuing a multitude of Department of Defense logistical support contracts, Ron is the CEO of SAWTST, a $9 Million a year company. His military experience had provided leadership qualities and had given him the ability to pursue things unimaginable 25 years earlier. Ron looks for well qualified, hungry employees. He knows the military logisticians are well skilled and have a great work ethic. He believes military service members are team players and motivated to achieve with little guidance. Today, Ron is proud to serve the Homes for Troops Foundation *and seeks out former service members for his company. His success allows him to serve as the co-chairman for the Logistics and Transportation for Georgia Minority Supplier Development Council (GMSDC) as well as a Cornerstone Member of the Georgia Chamber of Commerce. SFC Ronald Saxton, Ret, often speaks to local organizations, giving back to the local community and paying his good fortune forward by espousing the virtues of hard work and teamwork.*

Know Yourself

IT IS ESSENTIAL THAT YOU UNDERSTAND YOUR PERSONAL TRAITS AND CHARACTERISTICS THAT MADE YOU SUCCESSFUL IN THE MILITARY. Part of this understanding is an awareness of your personal environmental factors and a keen sense of timing in order to make your next move. Knowing yourself and where you are going are the best ways to determine your level of readiness for transition.

This chapter is an exploration of you and why you are desirable in the commercial world as a logistics professional. The most successful transitions occur when you match your traits, attributes and characteristics to the job market. Identifying your undiscovered corporate abilities, incorporating them to your resume and practicing interviewing will increase your probability of a successful transition.

> *"If you know the enemy and know yourself, you need not fear the result of a hundred battles."*
>
> **Sun Tzu** 孫子
> *The Art of War*

Honest introspection is not an easy task, but will prove valuable through this exercise. Three assessments are offered in this very important chapter to help gain insight to your level of readiness. They include:

- A **Characteristics Assessment** to gain an understanding of your military and undiscovered skills that will translate well to a career in logistics.

- An **Environmental Assessment** that will challenge your understanding on outside factors such as location, retirement, family, schools and faith. If you are married or have a significant other, it is highly recommended you both take the assessment. Afterwards, discuss any results that might warrant more detailed analysis to offer better alignment.

- A **Timing Assessment** to determine how ready you are to transition based upon the availability of time for planning or need for immediate action.

Desirability of Military Personnel in the Civilian Market

Civilian employers find the characteristics and attributes obtained from your military experience invaluable. Transitioning military of all ranks have marketable technical and leadership skills. Beyond leadership, your military experience has enhanced numerous personal attributes and provided core competencies including loyalty, respect, integrity, reliability, and team building. From a military perspective, you have led teams and can adapt to many different situations rapidly. As a team player, you know the weakest link is someone who needs help keeping the team moving forward. Additionally, as part of a military group you are educated and tech savvy, a quick learner, possess a security clearance, perform well under pressure, and are probably willing to relocate for advancement. These attributes make you very marketable to the commercial employer in the civilian market.[1]

Your predecessors have instilled a reputation for high quality attributes developed through military service. In fact, over 30 million veterans have come before you since World War II. These veterans have laid the foundation of this reputation through their skills and abilities. You need confidence to know that your skills and abilities from the service are directly applicable to the logistics career field and job market.

DoD contract and civil service environments desire these military characteristics as well. Your knowledge, contacts and understanding of military policy and procedure are vital to the defense contract organization. These characteristics, combined with your logistics skills and capabilities offer many career options after the military, as discussed in Chapter 4. Your challenge is to consider the job markets, properly align your skills and decide what opportunities you would like to pursue for your next career. Translating this information for the civilian employer is critical for your successful transition. The remainder of this chapter will provide assistance in this vital process.

Empirical Studies

Literally hundreds of companies are military friendly. The United States Automobile Association (USAA) hires veterans of all ranks and is perhaps one of the most veteran friendly companies in America today. Many logistics companies such as Union Pacific and CSX have a tradition of being military friendly. Numerous defense contracting companies such as L-3, General Dynamics, Booze Allen Hamilton, Lockheed Martin, CACI, and others, frequently hire former military personnel as well.[2]

A survey recently published by the Society for Human Resource Managers provides insight into employers and their thoughts on hiring former military personnel. Human resource professionals from across many different U.S. based companies and sectors provided the survey data and the findings were startling. On the upside, companies believe there are many benefits to recruiting and hiring veterans. The most commonly cited quality is a sense of responsibility and ability to see efforts through to completion. In fact, an overwhelming 97% of companies surveyed believe the veteran's strong sense of responsibility is their number one factor in hiring the military.[3] Interestingly, there are many companies that know you are well suited for logistics work based on your military experience and are eager to hire you.

Discrimination Rights:
eeoc.gov/eeoc/
publications/ada_
veterans.cfm

On the down side, some companies have misperceptions about the risks and challenges associated with hiring employees with military experience. Most noted is the concern that former military employees will need extra time to adapt to new workplace cultures. You may need to gravitate toward military friendly companies, many of which are logistics oriented.

The challenge is for you, the veteran, to speak the commercial vernacular to demonstrate your understanding of the job requirements. Thorough research of the companies and jobs you are applying for will provide the ability to demonstrate your knowledge of the position and how capable you really are.

Consider these misperceptions as you interact with recruiters and hiring managers. Understand their concerns and plan your answers to interview questions accordingly. By arming yourself, you will relieve concerns and frustrations during your discussions. Remember, the skills you have obtained in the past will carry you through your transition. You must be able to decompose, translate and relate your characteristics, core values, and logistical skills when you write your resume and when you are sitting at the interview table with the hiring manager.

Personal Characteristics

Character, derived from the word characteristic, refers to the essence of a person or thing. Character is the combination of qualities that makes us different from one another. Traits and attributes make up characteristics. You likely have many of the same personality traits since birth; such as being outgoing, reclusive, shy or social. Traits are generally innate and are often difficult to change. However, all types of traits can be of substantial importance. You just need to figure out what traits you have and how your traits add value to your future employer.

Attributes, as opposed to traits, are not ingrained. Attributes are learned over time and are based on external experiences. Attributes generally refer to a specific behavior or behaviors. Therefore, as a military service-member, you may have developed strong attributes during a challenging and difficult professional career or situation, such as combat or peace keeping operations. Attributes such as motivation and enthusiasm are examples of characteristics that may change with your life or professional experience. A person may be committed and/or have strong integrity. He or she may be loyal and/or hard working. These attributes lead to certain behaviors, which can be strong predictors of how one will respond to different stimuli in the work environment.

It is essential to know your traits and attributes as they define your personal characteristics and character. Understanding yourself to this level will help you determine what best suits you in a career. For example, do you enjoy working with other people or prefer working alone? You need to determine how well you perform under stress. It is essential to understand how the military service has shaped you and your attributes. You must be able to relay this critical information to your future employer. Let's explore and use this knowledge for success in your next career.

Core Values

In addition to your attributes, remember your services Core Values. People hear the words *Loyalty, Duty, Respect, Selfless Service, Honor, Integrity*, and *Personal Courage* all the time. Service members learn these values during their initial training, and they represent tremendous personal qualities. Core Values for each service are presented below in Figure 2.1. For the rest of the time you spend in the military, you live these values every day in everything you do, twenty-four hours a day, seven days a week. The question is: How do you relay these to the prospective employer? Demonstrate both your passion for these core values as well as your *individual* traits and attributes. Knowing yourself is the first step in doing so.

Service	Core Values
Air Force	Integrity First, Service Before Self, Excellence In All We Do
Army	Loyalty, Duty, Respect, Selfless Service, Honor, Integrity, Personal Courage
Coast Guard	Honor, Respect, Devotion to Duty
Navy/Marines	Honor, Courage, Commitment

Figure 2.1 | Service Core Values

Why Companies Want You!

In addition to your core values, your traditional military skills such as professionalism, leadership, confidence, positive attitude, communications and organizational skills are all highly desired by commercial companies. Know that many of these characteristics are required of a quality logistics professional. Arguably, the military has trained some of the finest leaders in the world. Forbes recently published the following reasons to hire veterans in Figure 2.2.

Quality	Description
Leadership	Platoon leader, group leader, team leader: military veterans work in a highly team-oriented and hierarchical environment. This means they know how to take orders – and when to give them.
Grace under pressure	If you're on the front lines in a war, you need to stay calm and function under extreme pressures. It makes some HR and management calamities look trivial – after all what we do is HR/people management, not ER.
Performance and results-oriented	When you're in uniform you have a mission, one on which lives may be dependent. Performance and results are non-negotiable. You know how to get things done and you do them.
Self-sacrifice	Self-awareness and self-sacrifice. Leaders in the military have to watch out for their teams first and themselves second, which is a leadership scenario not always encountered in the Fortune 500.
Communication and goal-setting	Effective communicators build teams. Leaders set goals and teams accomplish them. You can't have one without the other.

Figure 2.2 | Five Reasons to Hire Veterans[4]

By virtue of military service, you already know how to track issues on a daily, if not hourly, basis. You have had to reassign tasks to other service members, take or give fitness tests, and oversee weapons cleaning, all simultaneously. These organizational qualities are key for any successful logistics manager. It has been said that the difference between success and failure is based on whether you are highly organized or not. Are you?

Your Military Logistical Skills

As stated in Chapter 1, your logistical skills gained in the military are highly valued by commercial employers. An understanding of how to translate and apply your skills to the civilian sector is essential. Later in this book, you will gain an understanding of how your trained skills from your Navy Rating, Army and Marine Corps Military Occupational Skill (MOS), and Air Force Specialty Code (AFSC) relate to the civilian logistics sector. A prerequisite to this alignment is understanding how your skills relate to the other logistical functions being performed in the military. Figure 2.3 below depicts the primary logistical occupations in each service.

DoD Log MOSs, AFSCs and Ratings

Army
88 - Transportation Branch (TC)
89, 91, 94 - Ammunition CMF, Mechanical Maintenance
     CMF & Ordnance Branch (OD)
92 - Quartermaster Corps Branch (QM)

Air Force
2A - Aerospace Maintenance
2E - Comm-Elec/WireSystems Maintenance
2F - Fuels
2G - Logistics Plans
2M - Missile & Space Systems Maintenance
2P - Precision Measurement Equipment Laboratory
2R - Maintenance Management Systems
2S - Materiel Management
2T - Transportation & Vehicle Maintenance
2W - Munitions & Weapons

Navy
SH - Ship's serviceman
CS - Culinary Specialist
AE - Aviation Electrician's Mate
AO - Aviation Ordnanceman
AM - Aviation Structure Mechanic
LS - Logistics Specialist

Marine Corps
04 Logistics
11 Utilities
13 Engineer, Construction, Facilities, & Equipment
21 Ground Ordnance Maintenance
23 Ammunition and Explosive Ordnance Disposal
30 Supply Administration and Operations
31 Distribution Management
33 Food Service
35 Motor Transport
59 Electronics Maintenance
60/61/62 Aircraft Maintenance

Figure 2.3 | DoD Logistics MOSs, AFSCs and Ratings

DoD Logistical Functions

In review of each service, each occupational skill identifier can easily be mapped or organized into four functional groups (Supply, Transportation, Maintenance and Logistics Management). Figure 2.4 below maps many of the MOS, AFSCs and Navy Ratings to the broader military logistical functional groups. It is important to understand this alignment, as the functional groups will map to commercial opportunities later in Chapter 3. Some military career fields translate easily into the civilian logistical workplace.

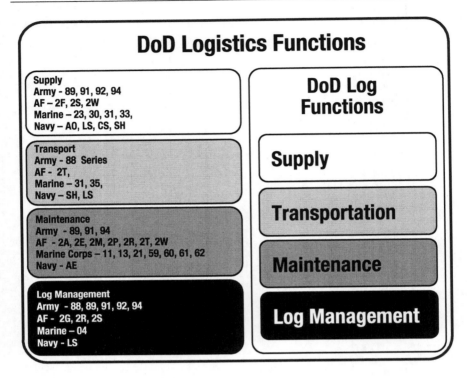

Figure 2.4 | DoD Logistical Functions

Military Logistics Management

Of the four logistics groupings, logistics management is unique in that managers from one of the other three functional groups often are promoted into this career field. Logistics management is in reach of most logistics leaders in the service. Regardless of rank, this is a career that you can aspire. Both commissioned and warrant officers from each service are trained in logistics management functions. Many NCOs reaching the grade of E7 or above, have obtained multi-functional logistics management experience. With certification, education and experience, the logistics management career field maybe a perfect professional goal to pursue. Figure 2.5 below depicts the typical service career levels that obtain logistics management experience in the DoD environment. Regardless, if you have been performing logistics management as an NCO, warrant officer or commissioned officer, your additional experience can be exploited for opportunities in the commercial world as elaborated in the sections below.

Careers in DoD Logistics Management Field	
Air Force	E5+ (In Some AFSCs), Officers
Army	E7+, Warrant Officers, Officers
Marine Corps	E7+, Warrant Officers, Officers
Navy	E7+, Officers

Figure 2.5 | DoD Logistics Management Fields

Non-Commissioned Officers

Soldiers, Marines, Sailors and Airmen are trained how to perform specific logistics duties after their initial training. As you were promoted to higher levels of responsibility as a NCO, you obtained considerable understanding of multi-functional military logistics. Most occupational skills at the senior NCO level feed the Military Logistics Management Group, as shown in Figure 2.5 above. One caveat is that some Air Force AFSC enter into service as logistic planners. These Airmen may be suitable for commercial logistics planning at the E5 level. However, their ability to obtain logistics management positions in the commercial world will depend on their leadership and service experience.

Warrant Officers

Warrant officers from the Army, Navy and the Marine Corps have very significant experiences in logistics management. Warrant officers have the virtue of being a specialist in a very specific logistical area while picking up the generalist functions of multi-functional logistics management. The best warrant officers have had to perform their specific specialty while educating themselves and learning other functions within logistics. Figure 2.6 below depicts the occupations of the Warrant Officer Corps within the Army and Marine Corps as they relate to the logistics management career field.

DoD Warrant Officer Logistics Career Fields

Army

880A Marine Deck Officer
881A Marine Engineering Officer
882A Mobility Officer
890A Ammunition Warrant Officer
913A Armament Systems Maintenance Warrant Officer
914A Allied Trades Warrant Officer
915A Automotive Maintenance Warrant Officer
915E Senior Automotive Maintenance Warrant Officer
919A Engineer Equipment Maintenance Warrant Officer
948D Electronic Missile Systems Maintenance Warrant Officer
948E Senior Electronics Maintenance Warrant Officer
920A Property Accounting Technician
920B Supply Systems Technician
921A Airdrop Systems Technician
922A Food Service Technician
923A Petroleum Systems Technician

Marine Corps

2110 - Ordnance Vehicle Maintenance Officer
2120 - Weapons Repair Officer
2125 - Electro-Optic Instrument Repair Officer
2305 - Explosive Ordnance Disposal Officer
2340 - Ammunition Officer
2805 - Data/Communications Maintenance Officer
3006 - Contracting Officer
3010 - Ground Supply operations Officer
3302 - Food Service Officer
5910 - Aviation Radar Maintenance Officer
5950 - Air Traffic Control Systems Maintenance Officer
5970 - Data Systems Maintenance Officer
6004 - Aircraft Maintenance Engineer Officer
6502 - Aviation Ordnance Office
6604 - Aviation Supply Operations Officer
6607 - Aviation Logistician
6608 - AIRSpeed Officer NMOS
8056 - Hazardous Material/Hazardous Waste
      (HM/HW) Officer
8057 - Acquisition Professional Candidate
8058 - Acquisition Manager/Acquisition Core Member
8060 - Acquisition Specialist
8862 - Material Management Officer

Figure 2.6 | Warrant Officer Career Fields

Commissioned Officers

If you are a commissioned officer, your career has probably taken on a multi-function logistics management flavor for much of your military experience. The majority of officers are trained on a specific logistics career field as a young officer. However, you quickly learn other logistics functions with professional development and on the job training during operations and exercises. Figure 2.7 below depicts the alignment of commissioned officer career fields across the services that make up the military logistics management grouping.

Regardless, your logistics management experience will vary significantly by individual military career path and assignments. You should relay these experiences to the commercial hiring manager. To assist with this translation, Chapter 3 will provide further mapping of your military logistical functions to the commercial logistics sector.

DoD Officer Logistics Management Career Fields

Army
90A Multifunctional Logistician
88A Transportation, General
88B Traffic Management
88C Marine and Terminal Operations
88D Motor/Rail Transportation
89E Explosive Ordnance Disposal Officer
91A Materiel Maintenance and Munitions Management Officer
92A Quartermaster Officer
92D Aerial Delivery and Materiel

Navy
Surface Warfare Supply Corps Officer (SWSCO)
Submarine Supply Officer
Naval Aviation Supply Officer (NASO)
Seabee Combat Warfare Officer
Navy Expeditionary Supply Corps Officer (NFSCO)

Air Force
20CO - Maintenance Group Commander or Deputy Group Commander
21RX - Logistics Readiness Officer (LRO)
21AX - Aircraft Maintenance Officer (MXO)
21MX - Munitions and Missile Maintenance

Marine Corps
1310 Engineer Equipment Officer
1330 Facilities Management Officer
1390 Bulk Fuel Officer
2102 Ordnance Officer
2110 Ordnance Vehicle Maintenance Officer
2120 Weapons Repair Officer
2125 Electro-Optic Instrument Repair Officer
2305 Explosive Ordnance Disposal Officer
2340 Ammunition Officer
3102 Distribution Management Officer
3302 Food Service Officer
3502 Motor Transport Officer
3510 Motor Transport Maintenance Officer
5902 Electronics Maintenance Officer (Aviation)
5910 Aviation Radar Maintenance Officer
5950 Air Traffic Control Systems Maintenance Officer
5970 Data Systems Maintenance Officer
6002 Aircraft Maintenance Officer
6004 Aircraft Maintenance Engineer Officer
0401 Basic Logistics Officer
0402 Logistics Officer
0405 Aerial Delivery Officer
0407 Personnel Retrieval and Processing Officer
0430 Mobility Officer
0477 Expeditionary Logistics Instructor (ELI)

Figure 2.7 | Commissioned Officer Career Fields

Communicating Your Characteristics to the Hiring Manager

Communication is critical when dealing with a hiring manager. You will only get a few minutes with them. Most will sum up an applicant within the first five minutes. Using your charisma and charm, let them know you are the best candidate for the job. Huge dividends will be paid to the candidate that learns all he/she can about the company and its operations, the future supervisor and hiring manager prior to the interview.

Translating your logistical knowledge, skills, abilities and experiences to the civilian marketplace is probably one of the most difficult challenges that you will face as you begin transition. There are a number of on-line translators to assist you in the development of your resume, based upon the skills and occupation you performed in the service. These are great tools. However,

Crafting an Elevator Speech:
mindtools.com

continue with this book and you will gain an understanding of your specific logistics skills and how to relate them to your future employer.

After you have written your resume and find yourself in an interview, make sure you do so with enthusiasm. Interlace discussions of your skills, flexibility, military traits, passion and trustworthiness to the hiring manager. Use personal experiences resulting in positive end-states. Always communicate your best characteristics reflecting the attributes you have. It is time to unfold your story with enthusiasm and relevance to the company. Hiring managers view this positively.

Superb tools for automatically translating your occupational skills civilian jobs!
military.com/veteran-jobs/skills-translator

Finally, unless specifically asked, never speak about your shortfalls. However, be prepared to answer the question, "Tell us about a time you failed". These are great opportunities to explain challenges that you have experienced. Explain the bad and the ugly. What is important is to show how you turned the situation around for the good and future efforts. You need a great answer in your hip pocket that indicates what you learned from the experience.

Assessment #1 *(Personal Characteristics)*

Three of five assessments in the book are in this chapter. Use these to gain insight on your personal transitional readiness, capabilities and potential growth areas.

Assessment #1, presented in Figure 2.8 challenges you to analyze your personal characteristics, values, traits and abilities. Read and answer each question. You can also utilize the companion guide to this book, available for download and print out on-line at **www.Gr8MilitaryLog.com**. When you are ready to analyze your assessment results, refer to Chapter 5.

1: Personal Characteristics

	Strongly Disagree	Disagree	Neither Agree OR Disagree	Agree	Strongly Agree
I enjoy working with and being around people familiar with logistics.					
I easily apply my logistical referential knowledge when performing tasks.					
I tend to lead a group when given the opportunity					
I can perform well in a stressful environment.					
I adapt quickly to changing environments.					
I enjoy being part of a team effort.					
I have the ability to learn concepts quickly					
I prefer working logistical operations.					
I take pride in briefing and reporting on my work.					
I proactively desire to learn and experience new concepts.					

Figure 2.8 | Personal Characteristics Assessment

Personal Environmental Factors

As you begin your transition it is important to understand your personal environmental factors. These factors affect you, your family, and your job opportunities. If you are like most, you will work after you transition from the military. If married, you certainly need to take into consideration your family's environmental requirements as you make decisions. Therefore, ensure you work through this section with them. If single, some of the considerations listed here may be relevant to your extended family or future plans.

Another factor to consider are your special family needs. Being close to extended family may constrain your job searching to certain geographic areas. Proximity to airports and hospitals might also need consideration.

There are many family issues to consider during your transition. Does your spouse need or want to work? Can they find jobs at the location you desire? Will he or she require more training or education? Will you or your family need to be near a university or college? Have you studied or discussed sharing your Post 911 GI Bill benefits with your family?

Location, Location, Location! - A phrase we are all quite familiar with. A critical consideration is moving to the location of your choice prior to your transition. It can be challenging and very expensive to get back to your U.S. home or to your desired location on your own dime, especially if overseas.

10 best places for military to retire
usaa.com/inet/
pages/enterprise_
bestplaces2013_
landing_mkt

You can save a tremendous amount of money if you can have the military get you back to your home of record, or if you can take your last assignment at your desired location. Another advantage to making this happen as part of your transition or retirement would be the ability to begin building your future local network early. If you know where you are going to end up, begin building your network remotely.

Here are some questions you should ask yourself if you have not already:

- *Have you considered the location of your next job?*
- *Have you looked at the weather as it relates to your health, hobbies and personal activities?*
- *What are the unemployment rate and the number of government related jobs for the local area?*
- *What is the cost of living?*
- *Do you have access to medical care or a Veterans Administration hospital?*
- *If you are leaving the service, do you have the need or desire to be near a military base so you can use the commissary, exchange and other facilities?*
- *Are you looking for a rural or urban life experience?*
- *Do you wish to live overseas?*
- *Do you understand the impact on you and your family with regard to the loss of military benefits?*
- *Do you know how much risk you and your family are willing to take with your next position?*

Assessment #2 *(Environmental Factors)*

The desire of Assessment #2, presented in Figure 2.9, is for you to perform a personal analysis of the associated environmental issues with your transition. As with the first assessment, read each question and choose the best answer. Refer to Chapter 5 when you are ready to analyze the results.

2: Environmental Factors	Strongly Disagree	Disagree	Neither Agree OR Disagree	Agree	Strongly Agree
I have analyzed and I am comfortable with the anticipated change associated with the loss of military benefits.					
I have determined my desired geographic location with regard to such factors as healthy lifestyle, allergies, health care access, hobbies, weather and entertainment.					
I have considered my family's special needs in my transition planning.					
I have performed a post-military financial analysis.					
I have given thought to my future location with regard to military base and/or VA Hospital proximity.					
I have studied transition locations with regard to extended family and transportation hub.					
I have analyzed my transition location with regard to future employment, taxation, real estate cost, and overall cost of living.					
I have considered my spouses occupation and their ability to find work.					
I have taken into account my children's primary, secondary and/or college education requirements.					
My family is supportive of my transition into another career					

Figure 2.9 | Environmental Factors Assessment

Timing

As in any transition, analyzing the timing of your departure is a key factor. With regard to your timing, this section includes an analysis of many elements, such as studying the educational benefits, developing and refining your resume, making interview preparations and approaching certification in the logistics field. The following timing related topics are presented as rhetorical questions for your comprehension, personal review and self-organization.

Is the Timing Right?

Are you ready to go? You do not want to regret your transition, as there is no going back if you still have something left to do in the military. There are many things to consider about timing. Gut instinct is probably not the best method for this determination. Looking at the associated timing issues and conducting self-assessments will likely provide a better result. These decisions should be made with a clear head and strong conviction. You may not be able to choose when to get off the bus, but you can choose to prepare yourself as best as possible. The bottom line – prepare with the limited time you have. Below are some things to consider when deciding if the timing is right to leave the service.

Are You Having Fun?

This may sound silly, but are you having fun in the military? Only you can determine if you are enjoying active duty. In general, active duty personnel truly enjoy the military lifestyle and the associated excitement. Many people look back at their time in service and remember their experience fondly. Others look back on the military as an accumulation of tough days. However, you should expect to have tough days in your civilian job. Some will remark, "Wow, did I do the right thing getting out?" Just remember, the grass is not always greener on the other side and choosing comfort over growth is not necessarily the correct choice.

Have You Achieved Your Personal Goals For Military Service?

Achieving your personal goals in the military can be quite challenging, especially today. You may have specific goals you were trying to obtain that are no longer attainable. You may also have a brilliant career ahead of you. Making the decision to get out of the service is always difficult. If you have accomplished your primary goals and objectives for military service, there is no need to fret about whether you should stay any longer. You may be painfully aware that you have obtained the highest rank possible. Remember, everyone gets passed over for promotion at some point. The military continually adjusts size based on the needs of the nation and the defense budget. The services have had to reduce their end-strengths in the past, are doing it now, and will do so again in the future. Everyone undergoes assessment and some will be involuntarily released from active duty. If this is your situation, be prepared and transition with a positive attitude.

Has A Good Transitional Job Opportunity Presented Itself?

Many veterans have stepped out of the service straight into great jobs. This occurs with some degree of frequency, but it is not the norm. Often your first job is "transitional". After being out a while, you realize that your first job is probably not the one you desire. Remember, you are just testing the waters when you first get out.

**COOL, Dude!
Certification
Information:**

cool.army.mil

cool.navy.mil

cool.navy.mil/usmc/usn

afvec.langley.af.mil/afvec/
Public/COOL

Regardless, if you desire to grow and develop you may have to move on.

Are You Prepared to Leave the Service?

Education and Certification

Do you need more skills or education prior to transitioning? The company that hires you does not always provide skills and education training. Organizations occasionally offer training; however, you may need to sign an agreement to pay back the training fees or commit to an additional time period. The military is a great environment for training and learning because of all the educational programs and opportunities available. Every branch of service offers some form of tuition assistance while on active duty. This lucrative benefit goes away upon transition and should be used prior to your departure from the service. Further, you may be able to get the service to pay for specialized logistics management or occupational certification training before departing. Each service has online guidance for credentialing and certification. Pursue these avenues with a great vengeance before departing service.

Finally, you should obtain a Post 911 GI Bill certificate of eligibility shortly after your transition and use that for you and your family's education.   If you have at least 90 days of aggregate active duty service after September 10, 2001, and are still on active duty, or if you are an honorably discharged Veteran or were discharged with a service-connected disability after 30 days, you may be eligible for this VA-administered program.

How is Your Financial Readiness?

Have you saved enough to survive the transition? These dollars need to be in short term savings and not locked up in a retirement account, so as to avoid penalties. The question becomes, "How much should you keep in a 'rainy-day' fund?" According to the Bureau of Labor Statistics, the rule of thumb of three to six months' worth of

Post 9/11 GI Bill
benefits.va.gov/gibill/
post911_gibill.asp

expenses may no longer apply. "A lot of experts now recommend that everyone keep nine months to one year of income in an emergency account in case of job loss," says Gail Cunningham, spokeswoman for the National Foundation for Credit Counseling in Washington, D.C.[5]

Have You Prepared Your Resume?

You need to know how to enhance and communicate your brand, including effective resume writing strategies. You want to avoid common resume "land-mines" or pitfalls frequently encountered by your fellow service members.

A powerful, impactful, well-written resume using civilian and business language, combined with the right format and branding power, can set you apart and propel you to a rewarding position in the private sector.

Be aware that commercial and civil service resumes can be very different. A few years ago, it was best practice to create a special resume with a specific format when applying for civil service positions. However, with the development of USAJOBS.gov, you can now upload your resume to this website and no longer use a resume builder for civil service jobs.

There is a definite skill to writing a resume. There are many tools and books to assist you with this. You will need to write and re-write your resume. Ask civilian hiring managers or people in the business to look at your resume. Stay away from other military service members, unless they have been in the civilian sector for a while. If you have money for professional preparation, this may be a good investment. You will need to modify the resume until you are comfortable with it. Many folks are surprised to hear that you often need to tailor your resume for the job you are applying for. Therefore, you may have multiple resumes for multiple lines of work. Do not limit your job search to your dream job. Getting the initial job after transition is more difficult than transferring to other jobs or positions. Apply for many jobs - start early and cast a wide net.

Need resume assistance:
resumegiant.co

It is recommended to post your resume on hiring sites like Monster.com, Indeed.com, and Career-Builder.com. These sites are scanned on a regular basis and you will get frequent emails informing you of opportunities. Even if the job is not exactly what you desire, apply. If you get an interview, pursue it and get a feel for the company and the position as it might be better than originally explained.

Common Resume Pitfalls

The following errors are often found in service member resumes as they prepare for transition. Watching out for these problem areas will increase the probability of your resume getting through the human resource staff screening and into the hands of the hiring official.

Resume is Written in Service Member Jargon

Examples include such terms as command and control, tactics, ISR, execution of battle plans, OPTEMPO, weaponry. There is no place for military jargon or vernacular in your civilian resume. Write your resume with your audience in mind. Most of the people scanning it are civilian human resources professionals who understand their industry and recruiting, not mortar ranges and targeting of terrorist networks. Focus on plain business language and your potential value to an employer.

Very Long Resume

A civilian resume should be two pages or less in length and communicate at an executive level. Do not try to cram 25+ years of military service into the resume. Instead, adjust your format and focus on your last 10-12 years. Employers will thank for you for this.

Resume with No Direction

"Operations Manager, Sales Manager, Director of Business Planning and jack of all trades." Do not let your resume display uncertainty or ambiguous career goals. Your resume should not float between work experience narratives with no central focus. You need to make a decision and decide what you want to place in your objective statement and write your resume to that. You can always change your mind with the next version of your resume or have multiple resumes, but you have to focus on one career direction per resume. Remember, you are telling a story and creating a brand for yourself. Your resume must show direction and tell your personal story as it relates to the position for which you are applying.

Job Duties Only

Often, a service member's first cut on a civilian resume focuses on the job duties performed. This makes sense as these are easily transferred from your military evaluations. However this technique does not work. Instead, you need to focus on achievements or impacts to show value and worth to your potential employer. By only listing job duties, you are telling a prospective employer you do not bring much to the table other than following direction.

For example, observe the following resume entry:

> Over 21 years of experience as a Manager. My emphasis has been, team and personnel development, logistics, ensuring soldier health and well-being, safety, production control and training management. Provided leadership and guidance to over 300 personnel in logistical, supply and commodities. Consistently exceeded production and operational goals of the company. Extensive practical experience in fleet maintenance and management, personnel, records, company operations and safety management.

A more succinct version of the above offers an executive message presenting the value you brought to the event, as follows:

> Fleet Maintenance Manager and principle advisor to Army executives on all logistics management functions within the organization. Directly influ-

enced military operational outcome through managing all maintenance and supply related activities, thereby ensuring readiness rate consistently higher than the Army standard of 90%. Ensured over 300 mechanics, supply and administrative workers were cross-trained, having them keep a clean and safe work environment; with an organizational record of 240 days. Constantly improved repair parts submittal process insuring error free orders, thereby saving the government over $17,000 dollars.

You need to show how you can help with the prospective company's strategy, financial goals, market penetration, and process improvements. Demonstrate you are more than an employee and that you are an asset to the team.

Winning Resume Strategies and Tips

To enhance and amplify your resume, you should focus on three major areas: branding, format and your specific achievements. The examples listed below are real world and have worked on numerous occasions.

Professional Branding

You are a professional brand. You might not necessarily realize this fact when you begin your transition, but it is true. Your civilian resume, LinkedIn® profile and job applications should all mutually support your common brand. Focus on key items like leadership or a subject matter expertise. Build a brand foundation that resonates throughout the resume. It is important to ensure your professional experience and education reflect who you are. Prospective hiring officials should have no doubt on your level of expertise and what you bring to the table. Make sure your Facebook and LinkedIn pages are strictly professional, as hiring professionals look at them.

Resume Format

When your resume gets in front of a recruiter or hiring manager, it has only around twelve seconds to do its job. Therefore, it needs to be clear and error-free. The three major formats are listed in Figure 2.10, below:

Resume Type	Description
Chronological	Starts by listing your work history. Jobs are listed in reverse chronological order with current, or most recent job, first. Employers typically prefer chronological, easy to see jobs held and when worked. Works well for job seekers with strong, solid work history.
Functional	Focuses on your skills and experience, rather than on your chronological work history. Used most often for changing careers or gaps in employment history.
Combination (Hybrid)	Lists skills and experience first. Employment history is listed next. Highlights relevant skills to the job you are applying for, while providing chronological work history that employers prefer.

Figure 2.10 | Resume Types[6]

Employers tend to favor a resume that is easy to follow and clearly communicates your professional track. If you plan on writing your own and have ten or more years of experience and education, selecting a format that concentrates on your assignments, accomplishments and education will be attractive to a corporate employer. Focus on your brand, with headline statements, executive profiles and your core competencies.

Resume Formats:
jobsearch.about.com

Achievements

Focus on both your achievements and career history, while highlighting your measurable capabilities and impact on the organization by personifying and enhancing your professional brand. It usually is around two pages with substantive data, achievements and branding features. You must show the impact you made on all previous positions. Listing that you had a job without any impact will not get you hired. Remember, they are hiring you and what you can bring to the table.

Have You Practiced Your Interviewing Skills?

Practicing interviewing is absolutely essential. Seek out and go on interviews regularly just to stay in practice. Interviewing is a very special skill. It takes a lot of time and finesse to be able to figure out the appropriate responses to the questions that your future employers are asking. Additionally, always be prepared to ask the hiring supervisor questions as well. This is a good indicator that you have done your homework and are showing an interest in what they do. Ensure you have studied the position description before the interview, so you can ask clarifying questions and gain more insight. Be honest during the interview. Do not overstate your capabilities. If you find you are not selected, you can and should ask why. If you make a mistake, you want to know so you can keep from making the same mistake again. Remember the adage, practice makes perfect. You can always inquire on other opportunities they know of within or outside their unit.

Have You Developed a Network?

Developing your network is a two-pronged attack. One must have a local network and an internet network. A great way to develop local networks is to volunteer at your local military association such as the Navy League, Association of the United States Army or Armed Forces Communications and Electronics Association (AFCEA). However, getting off the installation and meeting with local civilian organizations is a better way to expand your network. Find your closest Toastmasters Club. By way of example, the Tampa Bay Area has over 51 Toastmasters Clubs. Even better, there are numerous logistics organizations that you can get involved with around the country and potentially in your local area. Get started with the sampling of logistical networking organizations presented in Figure 2.11 below. These organizations and associations will not only offer national meetings, but often conduct regional and local chapter

Find local Toastmasters:
Toastmasters.org

meetings. Each one of these groups actively seeks volunteers. Volunteer and you will not only grow in your understanding of commercial logistics and enhance professional skills; you also actively increase your network. Some of these offer certification, which will be discussed more in Chapter 3.

Logistics Organization	Website
Air Transport Association of America	www.airlines.org
American Economic Association – AEA	www.vanderbilt.edu/AEA/index.htm
American Society of Transportation & Logistics, Inc. – ASTL	www.astl.org
American Trucking Associations, Inc. – ATA	www.truckline.com
Association of American Railroads	www.aar.org
APICS - supply chain and operations management	www.apics.org
Council of Supply Chain Management Professionals	www.cscmp.org
Council of Supply Chain Management Professionals – CSCMP	www.cscmp.org
Delta Nu Alpha	www.deltanualpha.org
Eno Transportation Foundation, Inc.	www.enotrans.com
Inland Rivers, Ports & Terminals, Inc.	www.irtp.net
Institute for Supply Management – ISM	www.ism.ws
Intermodal Association of North America – IANA	www.intermodal.org
International Association of Public Health Logisticians (IAPHL)	www.IAPHL.org
International Society of Logistics – SOLE	www.sole.org
Material Handling Industry of America	www.mhia.org
National Defense Transportation Association - NDTA	www.ndtahq.com
The Academy of International Business	www.aib.msu.edu
The Academy of Management	www.aomonline.com
The International Air Cargo Association	www.tiaca.org
The National Industrial Transportation League - NITL	www.ntil.org
Transportation Intermediaries Association – TIA	www.tianet.org
Transportation Research Board TRB	www.trb.org
Warehouse Education and Research Council	www.werc.org

Figure 2.11 | Professional American Logistics Organizations and Associations[7]

The International Association of Public Health Logisticians (IAPHL) is just one of these professional networking organizations that promote the professional development of supply chain managers, logisticians and workers in the public health logistics career field. IAPHL supports health care logisticians worldwide by providing a community of practice, where members network and improve their professional skills.[8] If you are working in or desire to work in health care logistics, this would be a perfect organization for you to seek out during your transition.

Just as important as developing a local network is developing your virtual network. Applications such as LinkedIn® are invaluable. Keeping in contact with friends and acquaintances through LinkedIn® is easy. Social media outlets are a great way to receive the latest news and opportunities. Further, members keep their addresses updated so there is no need for a massive annual address book update. This is a perfect method for keeping up with your professional acquaintances. If you have not done so already, create a LinkedIn® account and start building your online network as soon as possible.

EverNote® is another great application that works with your smart phone and LinkedIn®. Simply snap a photo of the business cards you collect from contacts and it automatically feeds your LinkedIn® Account. It is a great concept as more and more folks join LinkedIn®. The bottom line is that you need to network. It will pay huge dividends as you depart the service. Remember to start early.

Military Transition Web Sites:

Air Force:
afpc.af.mil/lifeandcareer/
transition.asp
Army:
acap.army.mil
Navy:
cnic.navy.mil/ffr/family_readiness/flee
_and_family_support_program/
transition_assistance.html
Marines:
mccscp.com/transition-assistance
veterans-benefits
Coast Guard:
uscg.mil/hr/cg111/transition_
assistance.asp

Transition Assistance Program

Finally, have you attended your local transition assistance program? These programs are absolutely essential for teaching you the basics needed for a successful transition. Transition information and counseling for pre-separation, employment assistance, relocation, education and training, health and life insurance, finances, reserve affiliation, disabled veterans, and retirement are provided. However, do not expect to find a job from this program.

SWOT Analysis

As another tool for your transition preparation and ability to know yourself, the Strength, Weaknesses, Opportunities and Threats (SWOT) analysis is presented. The SWOT analysis was originally developed for strategy and marketing and is used extensively by business developers. SWOT is a method for determining competitive advantage in the market place. Use this tool to help determine your competitive advantage in the job market competition. Performing a self-analysis to determine your abilities or challenges within these four areas will not only give you a greater understanding of yourself, but provide a level of confidence you need to be competitive. Figure 2.12 below depicts those characteristics or attributes common to military personnel based on their typical military experience.

Strengths	Weaknesses
Internal, positive aspects under your control to exploit:	Negative aspects you control and can improve upon:
- Military work experience (Ch. 2)	- Lack of work experience (Ch. 3)
- Education (Ch. 3)	- Lack of understanding of job market (Ch. 3)
- Tech knowledge (Ch. 2)	- Lack of civilian vernacular (Ch. 3)
- Transferable characteristics -communication, leadership, teamwork (Ch. 2)	- Negative self-image (Ch. 2)
- Personal attributes - ability to work under pressure, work ethic, etc. (Ch. 2)	- Negative misconceptions about former military (Ch. 1)
- Innate Military Core Values (Ch. 2)	- Lack of professional or career knowledge in Logistics (Ch. 3)
- Ability to assess and perform introspection on your capabilities (Ch. 5)	
- Ability to gain certification (Ch. 3)	
Opportunities	**Threats**
Positive, external conditions outside of your control that you can exploit:	Negative, external conditions you cannot control, but can reduce the effect:
- Growth in logistics career field (Ch. 1)	- Knowing your competition (Ch. 3)
- Military friendly companies (Ch. 1)	- Negative misconceptions about former military (Ch. 1)
- Opportunities available through further educational and certification (Ch. 3)	- Competitors with better job hunting capabilities (Ch. 2)
- Fields in need of military attributes (Ch. 2)	- Obstacles - lack of education and certification (Ch. 3)
- Opportunities available with greater preparation and self-knowledge (Ch. 3)	- Competitors with superior skills (Ch. 3)
- Opportunities by greater understanding of civilian career field and market place (Ch. 4)	- Failure to stay marketable (Ch.3)
- Networking with seasoned commercial logisticians (Ch.3)	

Figure 2.12 | SWOT Analysis

Assessment #3 *(Timing)*

In Assessment #3 (shown in Figure 2.13), you will look at personal preparedness and timing of your transition. As before, read each question and choose the best answer.

3: Timing	Strongly Disagree	Disagree	Neither Agree OR Disagree	Agree	Strongly Agree
I am ready to leave the military experience behind.					
I have met my career goals for the military.					
I am enjoying or looking forward to making plans for my military transition.					
My resume has been completed and reviewed by a civilian professional.					
I have established a network of professionals in and out of the service.					
I have saved several months salary for financial sustainment during transition.					
I have successfully attended a local military transition assistance program.					
I have successfully branded myself on LinkedIn, Facebook or with appropriate professional associations.					
I have practiced my interviewing skills.					
I have performed a personal SWOT analysis.					

Figure 2.13 | Timing Assessment

Knowing yourself is critical when competing in today's job market. Seek professional enhancement at every turn. Do not be afraid to reach out to new opportunities and analyze alternative paths. Try different angles and exploit those areas where you gain traction. The story below depicts one young woman who pursued numerous opportunities in logistics and exploited those that worked well for her.

Jamie Caro
Knowing Yourself

JAMIE CARO GREW UP AS A US NAVY BRAT TRAVELING AROUND THE WORLD WITH HER FATHER AND FAMILY. After high school graduation Jamie enlisted in the Air Force Reserves, being sworn in by her father. Not only did Jamie find the reserves exciting, but it assisted her with funding college and gave her a sense of involvement and belonging.

With the ongoing fight in the Middle East and her positive reserve experience, Jamie found herself desiring to serve the country in the effort. Shortly before graduation from college, Jamie approached an Air Force career counselor about going to OCS after graduation and flying jets, but they told her she was too short. This fact caused significant frustration for Jamie, but she did not let this challenge slow down her desire to grow professionally.

Two weeks after graduation, Jamie volunteered for active duty deployment to Bagram Airbase in Afghanistan with the Air Force. During her deployment, she worked in various logistics career field positions such as the warehousing of parts, driving forklifts, providing ramp services to cargo aircraft using aircraft K-loaders, building cargo pallets, manifesting flights and passengers, supply and air transportation logistics missions. This experience enhanced her baseline logistics experience, enabling her to learn more and paying forward to her career.

Enjoying her international experience, Jamie completed her enlistment, and through her interactions with her associates returned back to Bagram Airfield in Afghanistan as a contractor. Performing the same work, at the same location, Jamie was proud to serve the country and service members in combat, with a slightly bigger paycheck. Jamie began to learn complex logistical functions, including hazardous material handling and sensitive equipment management and control. After three and a half years in Afghanistan, Jamie returned back to the states and signed on as a con-

tractor with Jacob's Technology, in support of the Army Material Command's Logistics Support Activity (LOGSA) contract. She quickly learned about logistics Information Technology (IT) management while working at LOGSA in Huntsville, Alabama. With her education, experience and recent certification, Jamie moved to IBM as the contract changed hands. There she provided real world air transportation and supply chain logistics while gaining experience on IT systems and business analysis. Jamie was promoted to quality assurance lead with IBM and then as a project manager for the Managed Services Data Center (LOGSA) Information Technology Services (LITeS) Contract. Jamie believes her willingness to travel, logistics experience, security clearance and desire to learn have paid great dividends for her career. Her credo is to provide quality products and delivery to the clients, while ensuring attention to detail. Jamie will continue to pursue training and new experiences in the ever changing logistics automation world.

Commercial Logistics Basics

YOU CAN NEVER BE COMPLETELY PREPARED FOR YOUR TRANSITION FROM THE MILITARY. However, as you approach this exciting and inevitable event, one thing is certain: the more you understand yourself, your skillsets and how they relate to the commercial logistics career field, the higher your probability of success in landing the right position.

Utilizing military terminology and methods, you have performed numerous logistics functions during your time in the service. Some veterans have performed logistics functions such as armorer, munition officer, maintenance NCO, by assignment or additional duty. Others may have had formalized military logistics training and spent years in the career field.

The good news is that much of today's military uses terminology often found in the commercial logistics world, such as "Just in time delivery" and "Inventory in motion". You must be able to understand and use civilian logistics vernacular to obtain that first job. Further, you must be able to translate your message and your experiences into something meaningful that your prospective employer desires.

> *"I don't know what the hell this 'logistics' is ... but I want some of it."*
>
> - Admiral E. J. King

45

The purpose of this chapter is to enhance your understanding of the exciting career field of commercial logistics and align your existing skills and capabilities to this future career pursuit. The emphasis is on explaining and decomposing commercial logistics and its associated nuances, complexities and variabilities. Regardless of where you land after the service, your familiarity of commercial logistics obtained from this study, balanced by your existing military experience, will make you a more knowledgeable logistics professional.

There are two major sections in this chapter:

1. *"Background"* – This section provides a brief understanding of the military origins of logistics, a look at the career field growth expectations and the alignment with commercial logistics.

2. *"Understanding the Commercial Logistics Occupations"*– Broken into the four functional logistics career fields (supply, transportation, maintenance and logistics management). This section provides an understanding of the different occupations, career paths, certification, education and training.

Later in this chapter, there is a skills assessment, which will determine your potential readiness for transition based on your logistics Knowledge, Skills and Abilities (KSAs). This assessment will highlight your potential personal growth areas in logistics, which will then be addressed and monitored through your Personal Strategic Roadmap, presented in Chapter 5.

A key aspect of transitioning from one career to another within the logistics career field is gaining a comfort level by using the terminology transcending all industries, from manufacturing to retail, information technology, trucking, and warehousing, to name a few. To help with this, we offer the following aids later in the book:

- **Appendix A** - A basic "lexicon" is provided to enhance your understanding of key concepts and their correlation between military and civilian terminology.

- **Appendix B** – Logistics related certification organizations

- **Appendix C** – Alternative Logistics Career Fields

Logistics is a broad field, encompassing procurement, production, distribution, and disposal activities. Therefore you will find a great many opportunities with a variety of positions in a multitude of industries for logistic positions. Health care, retail, and manufacturing are just a few of the many industries that require logistics professional and workers. This is good news if you desire to grow and have varied experiences.

Background

The term *"logistics"* comes from the French word *"logistique"* or *"loger"* a derivation meaning to lodge. The Greeks had a similar word; *"logistikos"* derived from calculating or accounting.[1] The Oxford English Dictionary defines logistics as "the branch of military science relating to procuring, maintaining and transporting material, personnel and facilities."[2] Early use of a logistics title for a military administrator was *"Logista"* during the Roman and Byzantine Empire.[3] "It said that Dr. William Muller who was the first public instructor of military science at the University of Gottingen, planned to launch the book named "The Elements of the Art of War". It's here that the word "Logistics" in English language appeared for the first time."[4] Regardless of terminology and exact definition, logistics process and planning have been around for millennium and remain the bane or boon of both business and the battlefield. Logistics is the essential element in all successful military campaigns and business market strategies.

You have personally used logistics planning techniques for the execution of deployments, exercises, training and missions. Similar military logistics planning techniques were used by Alexander the Great, as his Army moved across Asia. Further, many have said that World War II provided the backdrop for the biggest logistics operation

> *"My logisticians are a humorless lot ... they know if my campaign fails, they are the first ones I will slay."*
>
> - Alexander the Great

ever attempted. The D-Day landing and force buildup involved millions of tons of supplies, thousands of ships, and hundreds of thousands of personnel. The logistics buildup in Kuwait before the invasion of Iraq has also said to be rem-

47

iniscent of the logistics techniques used by the U.S. Army in World War II and repeated in the Korean War and the Gulf War of 1991.[5] During Operation Enduring Freedom, the challenges of logistic support in mountainous Afghanistan with poor road network cannot be overstated. Time sensitive logistic support had to be transported by air, with tenuous contracted surface transportation employment, in an effort to maintain redundant logistical systems.[6]

What you know about military logistics will serve you well in the commercial market place. Commercial and military logistics have much in common. The optimistic military "can do" motto has a similar corollary in commercial logistics: "Having the right item, in the right quantity, at the right time, at the right place, for the right price, in the right condition, to the right customer". However, you must understand distinctions between military and commercial logistics. To gain a better understanding, let's take a look at some of the differences between military and commercial logistics. Later, we will look for similarities when we discuss career field alignment.

Profit

The first major distinction is profit. Just like the military, a logistician must get the product and services to the proper location, when the customer desires. However, in the commercial world you must also perform these activities in the most efficient method, at the lowest cost possible, thereby maximizing company profit. You should understand that there is a difference in the commercial world, because of the profit motive and competition. Therefore, it is important to understand the profit motive and how to assist your company in its most important goals; making money and remaining competitive.

Commercial Logistics Organizations

Knowing where you will work within the logistical career field is important. As you enter into the commercial job market, you may work for a logistics company, such as a trucking company or shipping line, air transporter, or freight forwarder. However, there are many companies (manufacturing and sales) that have logistics sections or branches. This can be an extremely lucrative career sector as well and could become your first home after the service.

Government Logistics Organizations

Often differentiated by lack of profit motive, federal and local governments all have a multitude of logistics and logistics management positions. You may be best suited working for a federal department or administration, or a state, county or city government as a logistician. This may be an extremely rewarding career sector for you after the service. This market place and associated rewards and challenges will be discussed in Chapter 4.

Terminology Nuance

As logistics has grown, terminology has become more complicated and confusing. As an example, terms like operations or production management in the commercial environment, generally refer to a manufacturing or physical transformation, taking place at a single business location such as a restaurant, bank or production facility. While products are ready for consumption in the factory, you must transport product to the correct location. In commercial industry, the term logistics relates to such activities as distribution and moving products. There are similarities between operations management and logistics, which can add confusion.

Terms for hybrid professionals, such as "Director of Operations" or "Logistics Officer" are often used interchangeably for work on the same effort. Furthermore, the term supply chain management indicates a global perspective in both production and logistics from point of origin, to point of production, to point of sale.

While confusing, clarity can be obtained with a general understanding of terminology. To gain a better understanding and learn some more of the vernacular, use the lexicon found in Appendix A. Appendix C provides high level definitions of commercial alternative logistics fields such as procurement logistics, distribution logistics, Reliability, Availability and Maintainability (RAM) logistics.

Outlook

As mentioned earlier in the book, the logistics career field has a positive outlook. As the industry continues to enjoy unfettered global growth, the median pay for logistician managers with a bachelor's degree is around $72,780 per year. Further, the outlook through 2025 indicates 21% growth, far better than the national outlook average of 11%.[7] Warehouse workers and truck drivers should meet the national average growth rate. Understandably, not all occupations within the logistics career field will enjoy this positive outlook. For example, purchasing managers and material clerks are not predicted to keep up with the average growth rate. Figure 3.1 below, extracted from the Bureau of Labor and Statistics, depicts sample occupations, with their average salaries, expected growth rate and current number of jobs nationwide.

Job Title	Salary	Growth Rate	Number of U.S. Jobs
Logistician	$72,780	22%	125,900
Warehouse Laborer	$22,970	10%	3,428,800
Material Recording Clerks	$24,810	1%	2,859,500
Tractor-Trailer Truck Drivers	$38,200	11%	1,701,500
Delivery Truck Drivers	$27,530	5%	1,273,600
Purchasing Managers	$60,550	4%	504,600
Truck Mechanics	$45,160	1%	243,080

Figure 3.1 | Sample Occupation Salaries and Growth

Career Field Alignment

Obviously, logistics has been around for many years in commercial industry. Due to the increasing challenges of supplying businesses with the right materials at the right place at the right time, logistics has become increasingly complex in the globalization of our world. The Council of Supply Chain Management Professionals defines logistics as "The process of planning, implementing, and controlling the effective and efficient flow of goods and services from the point of origin to the point of consumption." With no mention of maintenance, we can begin to see the differences between military and commercial logistics. Therefore, supply and transportation are the essence of commercial logistics. Military supply and transportation veterans generally flow well into their respective commercial functions.

However, one of the distinct differences between military and commercial logistics is the recognition of maintenance as a separate and distinct logistic career field by the Army and Marine Corps. By contrast, commercial companies perform maintenance functions, but do not recognize mainte-

> *"Supply and transport stand or fall together: history depends on both."*
>
> - Winston Churchill

nance as a logistics function. You can perform maintenance and maintenance management in the commercial world, but maintenance is not typically considered to be soley a logistics career field occupation. Therefore, maintenance has the luxury of being performed in both of the logistics career fields of supply and transportation, while feeding numerous other commercial fields as well.

Reflecting back on the military logistics grouping given in Chapter 2, Figure 3.2 below depicts the relationship of the military logistic functions to the commercial logistic functions.

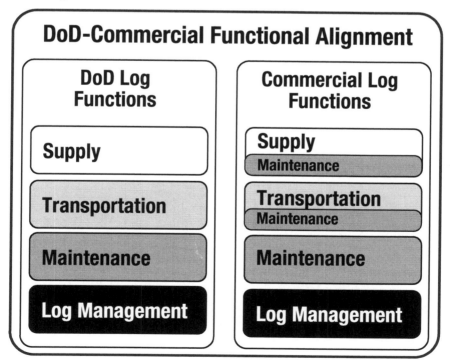

Figure 3.2 | DoD - Commercial Logistics Functional Alignment

Once you understand how the military logistics functions flow into the commercial functions, you can begin to unravel the relationship to the commercial logistics career fields and the respective occupations. Figure 3.3 shows the basic alignment of the high level career fields within commercial logistics and example occupations.

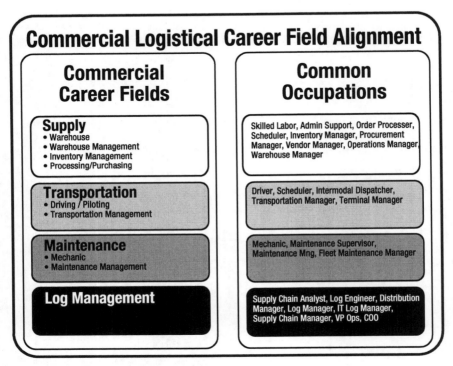

Figure 3.3 | Commercial Logistical Career Field Alignment

Military supply and transportation veterans with enough experience and education can transition into the commercial logistics management field and it is certainly a possible commercial career field move. Maintenance managers can also feed commercial logistics management, if they have logistics support operations training and experience. Therefore a significant number of NCOs are great candidates for this profession. Logistics management tends to be cross functional with a wider view of the operations and total logistics function of the organization.

Do you have enough management experience and can you portray your capabilities well enough to the recruiter to obtain the managerial job? The next section will depict occupational background information for you as you study and assess yourself during your transition.

Understanding Commercial Logistics Occupations

This section relates a basic understanding of common logistics occupations. As stated earlier, the chapter concentrates on four functions; supply, transportation, maintenance and logistics management. When possible, experience, education, and relevant certifications are given for each career field.

Supply and Supply Management

It is difficult to not speak about supply chain when discussing supply. Jaquelin Smith, a Forbes Staff writer, recently penned the Article *"The Happiest Jobs In America"*. She stated that CareerBliss® had compiled a list of the 20 happiest jobs based on analysis from more than 100,400 employee-generated reviews, and that the warehouse manager was the 4th happiest job in America.[8] SCDigest anecdotal conversations with supply chain recruiters indicate that after a couple tough years following the recession in 2008, demand for supply chain talent continues to outpace available workers. The actual supply chain is a system of organizations, people, activities, information, and resources involved in moving a product or service from supplier to customer. Every function and every step is based upon the supply chain for a particular product or products. Typically, workers in the field of supply are helping to move supplies along the supply chain.

One of the major focal points in the supply chain is the warehouse. Time and distance between nodes is always a factor, but streamlining warehouse functions seems to be a perennial discussion. In the commercial world, there are basically three types of warehouses; supply, trans-shipment and distribution. These are described in Figure 3.4 below.

Warehouse Type	Description
Supply	Usually part of production operation. Raw materials housed here along with auxiliary supplies needed for the production. Sometimes you'll find products that are nearly completed and goods used in production processing.
Trans-shipment	Keeps goods for shorter periods of time, when they are in transit or ready to be transferred from one means of transportation to some other conveyance. Building often has two loading docks, one on each side of the building. As product or supply moves in one side and into another conveyance on the other side of the building for onward movement to another location within the country.
Local Distribution	Goods are going to be distributed in the local region. Also known as a central, regional or local distribution warehouses, or delivery warehouse. Regardless, goods from production are stored before delivery to customers, usually locally or regionally.

Figure 3.4 | Warehouse Types and Descriptions

Within the supply chain and warehouses, there are many management systems. Employees will be engaged working or managing these systems and have a specific function within the supply chain. Generally, military supply workers transition into commercial supply easily due to their skills and training in the service. Therefore, if you like working as a warehouse associate or order processor, you are probably well suited for these commercial occupations. As your training and experience grow, there is a no singular definitive career ladder within this career field. However, you will generally need to be an inventory, procurement and or vendor manager to become an operations manager, which can all lead to supply chain or logistics management career fields. Sample supply career fields are given in Figure 3.5 below and described in the next pages.

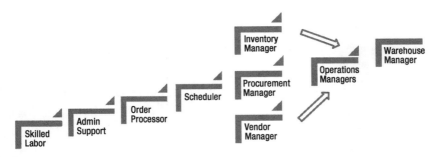

Figure 3.5 | Supply Career Ladder

Skilled Labor

Also known as warehouse associates, these valued team members are forklift operators, material handlers and tractor trailer drivers. They are needed to move and transport product from alternate inventory locations. On any given day, an associate may find themselves loading and unloading stock, maintaining clean and orderly warehouse, packing and labeling items for shipment, and performing minor assembly.

Administrative Support

These instrumental team members handle the day-to-day clerical and support functions of the warehouse, comprising a wide variety of positions in the areas of customer service, data entry, contracts and accounting. Other positions that fall in this category are dispatching, inventory and safety administration, HAZMAT and packaging technicians.

Order Processor

Order processors take orders from customers and input them into the company's system for dispatch. This position requires attention to detail and the ability to work quickly. A job as an order processor can be a good way to get your foot in the door with a larger company and learn how it works from inside. Processors typically take orders directly from customers over the phone, by fax or through email. Most order processing now is electronic, so computer experience is essential. Order processors should be familiar with software programs such as Microsoft Office and the use of spreadsheets. Although not necessary, knowledge of databases such as SQL can also be helpful.[9]

> *"Leaders win through logistics... when you go to war, you need to have both toilet paper and bullets at the right place at the right time...."*
>
> - Tom Peters

Scheduler

In the warehouse, schedulers prioritize inbound and outbound shipments to make sure that it gets to the end user in a timely matter. They ensure there is ample supply to ship, organize materials and transportation and make sure schedules are created and kept.

Inventory Manager

The inventory manager determines appropriate stockage objectives in an effort to minimize total operating costs yet satisfy customers' requirements. The inventory manager needs to ensure he/she understands the importance of customers demand, your company's different product(s), quality, transportation policies and capabilities and production, while maintaining knowledge of your competitors and their capabilities. Properly documenting and accounting will also help your company avoid inventory imbalance due to loss or theft. Purchasing, negotiating and signing contracts with suppliers may be part of your responsibility, depending on the size of your company.

Procurement Manager (Purchaser)

Procurement managers work for large companies and are in charge of managing and coordinating procurement agents, buyers or purchasing agents, as well as working on the most complex purchases for the company. They research, evaluate and buy products for companies to either resell to customers or for use in their everyday operations. They also determine what products get to store shelves, in catalogues, and online. They research and create the deals to buy large quantities of products for their companies.

Vendor Manager

As a vendor manager, you develop and maintain strategic relationship with suppliers. You will evaluate and build relationships with good, high quality suppliers. You will appraise their ability to communicate and deal with your companies concerns and problems, such as a delay in an order being processed. You will need to be constantly searching for and be aware of other suppliers who may be willing to provide your business with materials at a better cost.

Additionally, as vendor manager, you should be consistently seeking suppliers and vendors that will be low cost, high quality; while you protect the bottom line of the company.

Operations Managers

As a warehouse operations manager, you are responsible for overseeing all aspects of the warehouse. You need the ability to plan and oversee transportation systems, lead and motivate a team, prepare and maintain a financial budget and handle customer concerns. Operations managers must ensure the warehouse adheres to Occupational Safety and Health Administration (OSHA) guidelines. You will plan a weekly activity forecast based on such factors as statistics and trends, while having team leaders working to get the job done by the most effective means.

Warehouse Manager (Supervisor)

Warehouse supervisors are in charge of most functions of the warehouse and inventory. Warehouse supervisors lead a team of inventory or warehouse workers to receive and record new stock as it comes in, and move stock onto trucks or store shelves as needed. Warehouse supervisors interview and hire employees, create schedules, monitor stock levels at the warehouse and know when to replenish stock. Depending on the job, warehouse supervisors may have similar duties to a scheduler or logistician.

Liquid Supply Field Considerations

In addition to moving dry goods, it is important to note that there is certainly room for military fuel and water specialists in the commercial world. Liquid supply is a significant career field when millions of gallons of bulk fuel, water, juice, chemicals and milk are moved daily in this country. Fuel storage terminals and liquid warehouse facilities are in every city and are certainly looking for certified personnel. Another form of liquid supply is pipeline logistics. If you have experience in receiving, stocking and issuing bulk fuels and water at storage and distribution facilities, selecting and submitting samples for laboratory testing and performing petroleum and water accounting duties, you may want to get civilian certifications and pursue this career field.

Supply Certifications

Fortunately for you as a transitioning service member, you now have many free and low cost options available to help you gain certification. Further, a significant amount of training is available to you before you leave the service. It is highly recommended that you explore the different options and take the available online courses. Additionally, funds for training and testing reimbursement are available to you after you leave the service from the Veterans

Administration and GI Bill. Regardless, take advantage of every opportunity for education as soon as you can. Appendix B provides a listing of certification organizations and their associated web addresses.

Army

Through the Army Credentialing Opportunities Online (COOL) program, enlisted soldiers can learn about various supply certifications available, alignment of their MOS to the certifications and resources to receive reimbursement and training for the supply related certifications. Many of these have the exam approved for payment through the G.I. Bill. In some cases, the COOL Website has state-of-the-art computer-based training available, free to the army workforce. Certification information available through Army COOL for the 92 Series MOS is listed in Figure 3.6 below.

ARMY - Supply Certification	Certifying Body
Certified Facility Manager	International Facility Management Association (IFMA)
Certified Fellow in Production and Inventory Management (CFPIM)	APICS The Association for Operations Management
Certified in Production and Inventory Management (CPIM)	Certified in Transportation and Logistics (CTL)
American Society of Transportation and Logistics, Inc. (AST&L)	Certified Logistics Associate (CLA)
Manufacturing Skill Standards Council (MSSC)	Certified Logistics Technician (CLT (AE)
Certified Manager (CM)	Institute of Certified Professional Managers (ICPM)
Certified Manager of Quality/Organizational Excellence (CMQ/OE)	American Society for Quality (ASQ)
Certified Packaging Professional	Institute of Packaging Professionals (IoPP)
Certified Professional in Supply Management (CPSM)	Institute for Supply Management (ISM)
Certified Professional in Training	Institute of Packaging Professionals (IoPP)
Certified Professional Logistician (CPL)	The International Society of Logistics (SOLE)
Demonstrated Logistician	
Distinguished Logistics Professional (DLP)	American Society of Transportation and Logistics, Inc. (AST&L)
Global Logistics Associate (GLA)	
Professional Designation in Logistics and Supply Chain Management (PLS)	

Figure 3.6 | Supply Certifications Information From Army COOL

Navy, Marine Corps, Air Force COOL

The Services all have websites similar to Army COOL Website, with varying degrees of maturity. Some exceptions include free on-line computer training capability. Figure 3.7 below describes the certification information available from Navy COOL for supply personnel.

NAVY COOL - Supply Certification	Certifying Body
Certified in Production and Inventory Management (CPIM)	APICS The Association for Operations Management
Certified Logistics Associate (CLA)	Manufacturing Skill Standards Council (MSSC)
Certified Logistics Technician (CLT (AE))	Mail Systems Management Association
Certified Mail and Distribution Systems Manager (CMDSM)	In-Plant Printing and Mailing Association
Certified Mail Manager (CMM)	Institute of Certified Professional Managers (ICPM)
Certified Manager (CM)	The International Society of Logistics (SOLE)
Certified Master Logistician (CML)	Institute for Supply Management (ISM)
Certified Professional in Supply Management (CPSM)	The International Society of Logistics (SOLE)
Certified Professional Logistician (CPL)	Universal Public Procurement Certification Council (UPPCC)
Certified Professional Public Buyer (CPPB)	Certified Supply Chain Professional (CSCP)
Certified Supply Chain Professional (CSCP)	APICS The Association for Operations Management
Demonstrated Logistician	The International Society of Logistics (SOLE)
Global Logistics Associate (GLA)	American Society of Transportation and Logistics, Inc. (AST&L)

Figure 3.7 | Supply Certifications Information From Navy COOL

Transportation and Transportation Management

According to an ABC News special on 20/20, truck driving is not a job or a career, it is a lifestyle. Being a line haul trucker and the associated lifestyle are not for everyone. But for those that love the open road, it is second to none. During the special, driver Loren West stated, "I enjoy posting pictures and videos of the views from my 'office window' on my Facebook page."[10]

In today's global economy, drivers and operators are in more demand than ever. All transportation conveyances such as train, trucking, boats, airplanes companies, are needed in the industry. Couriers, freight forwarders and multi-modal transport operators are just some of the many areas for transporters. Generally military transportation workers readily transition into commercial transportation. Therefore, if you desire to continue working as a truck driver, you are probably well suited for commercial occupations. However, if you desire to grow into a managerial position with the transportation career field, there is certainly opportunity for former military service members.

There are usually multiple types of transportation hubs: sea-road, sea-rail and road-rail, and sea-road-rail. With the growth of containerization, intermodal freight transport has become more efficient. Your knowledge, leadership and management skills are needed.

Similarly to the supply section above, as you mature in the career field of transportation management, there are many career ladders for you to follow, leading to logistics management. A sample transportation career ladder is given in Figure 3.8 below and described in the next pages.

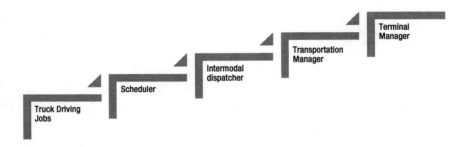

Figure 3.8| Transportation Management Career Ladder

Local Driving

Local driving includes such areas as home delivery, flatbed delivery, and traditional van delivery are among the positions available as are straight truck and Class B delivery opportunities. This work requires a combination of customer service, material handling, installation and driving duties. If you prefer to focus on driving, you will enjoy more home time as a local truck driver.

Over The Road / Linehaul

If you have obtained or desire to obtain your professional truck driver certification and enjoy the trucking lifestyle, but also need some time at home, regional trucking may be a perfect balance for you. Many companies offer weekly or biweekly home time, offering a nice balance of driving duties and time off. Regional truck driving opportunities are available in almost all regions of the country. Regardless, regional truck drivers are usually home weekly or biweekly.

Owner Operator

If you like entrepreneurship, and have a knack for running a business, owner operators will enjoy maximum flexibility with highest reward in the trucking industry. Having good pay and constant loads are highly desirable, and most major corporations can offer this to an owner operator. Many larger corporations offer benefits including reduced cost on parts and maintenance, while providing access to reduced group rates on voluntary health, dental, prescription and vision plans.

Lease Purchase Trucking

Often a company will offer a lease-purchase program for drivers who desire to own their vehicle. This comes with advantages, but you are generally still beholden to the company you make the agreement with.

Scheduler

The scheduler coordinates and schedules efficient and effective flow of transportation assets for the company, maximizing loads for conveyance, while ensuring on-time delivery. The scheduler provides support to the dispatch staff and ensures availability of tools and automation assets.

Intermodal Dispatcher

The Intermodal Dispatcher schedules, dispatches and updates records for status of goods, while interacting across departments and with federal and international customs groups. They enter data and update dispatch logs for transport of goods and audit safety of transportation modes, including driver certifications.

Transportation Manager

Transportation managers oversee the loading, storage, packaging and transportation of goods. Their main responsibility is to make sure things get where they need to go, but they are also responsible for controlling expenses, limiting damages and ensuring transport operates within the law. This career field is a definite feeder for a logistics management career.

Terminal Manager

Terminal managers oversee the terminal's operations. Duties typically include coordinating freight, verifying and reviewing paperwork such as bills of lading, assigning responsibilities to employees, enforcing compliance policies and communicating with customers to provide updates and resolve issues.

Transportation Certifications

If you are considering driving a truck and if you do not already have a CDL, you must pursue it soon. Fortunately, as a transitioning service member, you now have many free and low cost options available to help you gain certification. Further, a significant amount of training is available to you before you leave the service. "Troops to Trucks", a recent initiative, is assisting military trained truck drivers receive their CDL.[11] This process, which is streamlined through a new federal regulation, gives service members a waiver for the road skills test. A written test will still be required. There are also discussions about Army MOS 88N (transportation movement coordinator) receiving certification in the area of Freight Forwarding.

Army e-Learning:
usarmy.skillport.com

If applicable, make sure to use your Army E-learning benefit prior to getting out. A multitude of courses in management exist on this site. It is recommended that you explore the different options and take the available online courses.

Army and Navy COOL are other methods for gaining information regarding commercial certifications. Through Army COOL enlisted soldiers can learn about various transportation certifications, the alignment of their MOS to the certifications, and resources to receive reimbursement for the training needed for certification. Many of these have the exam approved for payment through the G.I. Bill. In some cases the COOL Website has state-of-the-art, computer-based training available, free to soldiers. Certification information available through Army COOL for 88 Series is listed in Figure 3.9 below.

Transportation Certifications	Credentialing Body
Commercial Driver License (CDL)	Department of Transportation
Certified Director of Safety (CDS)	North American Transportation Management Institute (NATMI)
Certified Director of Maintenance/Equipment (CDM/E)	
Certified Safety Supervisor (CSS)	
Certified Supervisor of Maintenance/Equipment (CSM/E)	
Certified Driver Trainer (CDT)	
Certified Cargo Security Professional (CCSP)	

Figure 3.9 | Army COOL - Transportation Certification Information

Navy, Marine Corps, Air Force COOL

The Services all have websites similar to the Army COOL Website, with varying degrees of maturity. Some of the sites include a free on-line computer training capability. Figure 3.10 Transportation Certifications Credentialing Body below describes the CDL certification information available from the Air Force COOL Website for Air Force transportation personnel.

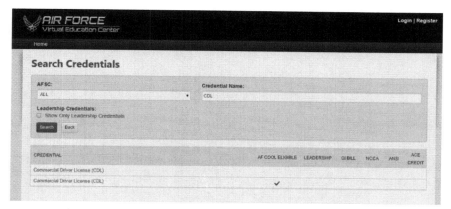

Figure 3.10 | Air Force COOL - Transportation CDL Certification Information

Also remember that funds for training and testing reimbursement are available to you after you leave the service from the Veterans Administration and GI Bill. Regardless, take advantage of every opportunity for education as soon as you can, prior to leaving the service if possible. Additionally, Appendix B provides a listing of certification organizations and their associated web addresses.

Maintenance and Maintenance Management

Job Shadow, an online information provider for commercial job seekers, recently interviewed an auto mechanic for a car dealership. When asked "What is most rewarding about this job?" the mechanic stated, "struggling to figure something out and then finally completing the repair successfully is pretty rewarding. That's about it, it's not like anyone 'thanks' a mechanic, not that I expect it."[12] On a positive note, mechanics are in demand. Even though the job does not pay as well as other sectors, it is steady 9-5 work available everywhere. In a recent online salary article, the author stated, "...Americans are looking for reliable, stable employment opportunities. Automotive Service Excellence (ASE) certification can give you the keys to a rewarding career. The demand for mechanics and technicians has given thousands of hard working Americans a reliable paycheck."[13]

As a mechanic, there are many companies with which you can find work. Organizations generally perform maintenance on company owned equipment by either organic or third party mechanics. Leasing companies normally maintain their equipment at the leasing facility. However, the leasing company may provide onsite mechanics or contact teams. A good example of the contact team is the maintenance of Material Handling Equipment (MHE) in the warehouse environment.

A battalion maintenance NCO may be a perfect fit as a maintenance supervisor at a transportation terminal for a company like Schneider or YRC Trucking. You would probably have organic or out-sourced mechanics, schedulers and procurement specialists working for you.

As a mechanic or maintenance manager you will need to seek out job listings and hiring officials at these different organizations. As you grow and mature in the career field of maintenance, there is a career ladder for you to follow which can lead to logistics management. A sample maintenance career ladder is given in Figure 3.11 below and described in the next pages.

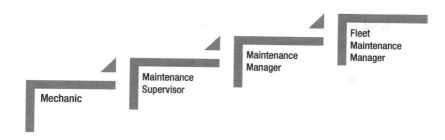

Figure 3.11 | Maintenance Career Ladder

Mechanic

Mechanics are in charge of maintaining company-related machinery. They are responsible for providing upkeep to that machinery to ensure that needed equipment functions properly; this includes preventive care and maintenance. Mechanics perform regular inspections to ensure machines comply with local, state, and federal regulations.

Maintenance Supervisor

As a maintenance supervisor, you will provide direction to maintenance technicians while ensuring all maintenance work is performed on time, safely and efficiently, using internal resource allocation as needed.

Maintenance Manager

Maintenance managers provide direction to on-site maintenance technicians and technician supervisors, and leadership and direction to maintenance supervisors or maintenance managers, to ensure that all repair/ maintenance work is performed in a safe, efficient and timely manner, reallocating resources among sites as appropriate. Additionally, the maintenance manager oversees the coordination, planning/ scheduling of all repair work to increase productivity, while effectively managing department's overtime. They monitor the shops' operational performance and efficiency; take action to redirect activities appropriately. Interestingly, the maintenance manager may also oversee all consumable Petroleum, Oils and Lubricants (POL) in a terminal situation. The maintenance manager may report to the fleet manager or in some cases the terminal manager.

Fleet Maintenance Manager

The fleet maintenance manager is responsible for overseeing multiple maintenance shops and managing multiple teams of technicians (mechanics), maintenance supervisors and/or other maintenance managers who are responsible for the preventive maintenance and repair of a fleet of vehicles. He or she provides direction through multiple maintenance supervisors, to a group of technicians and for implementing and monitoring maintenance policies and procedures to ensure that all repairs and maintenance to trucks, containers, trailers and other heavy duty equipment are performed within compliance standards and all federal and state regulations.[14]

Maintenance Certifications

Fortunately for you as a transitioning service member, you now have many free and low cost options available to help you gain certification. Further, a significant amount of training is available to you before you leave the service. It is recommended that you explore the different options and take the available online courses. Additionally, funds for training and testing reimbursement are available to you after you leave the service from the Veterans Administration and GI Bill. Regardless, take advantage of every opportunity for education as soon as you can. Also be sure to review Appendix B, which provides a listing of certification organizations and their associated web addresses.

Army

Through the Army Credentialing Opportunities Online (COOL) program, enlisted soldiers can learn about various supply certifications available, alignment of their MOS to the certifications, resources to receive reimbursement and training for the supply related certifications. Many of these have the exam approved for payment through the G.I. Bill. In some cases, the COOL Website has state-of-the-art, computer-based training available, free to the army workforce. Certification information available through Army COOL for the 91 maintenance series is listed in Figure 3.12 below.

Navy, Marine Corps, Air Force COOL

The Services all have websites similar to Army COOL website, with varying degrees of maturity. Some exceptions include free on-line computer training

NAVY COOL - Maintenance Certification	Credentialing Body
Auto Maintenance and Light Repair Certification Test (G1)	National Institute for Automotive Service Excellence (ASE)
Autodesk AutoCAD User Certification	Autodesk
Automobile Service Consultant (C1)	National Institute for Automotive Service Excellence (ASE)
Automobile/Light Truck - Automatic Transmission/ Transaxle (A2)	
Automobile/Light Truck - Brakes (A5)	
Automobile/Light Truck - Electrical/Electronic Systems (A6)	
Automobile/Light Truck - Engine Performance (A8)	
Automobile/Light Truck - Engine Repair (A1)	
Automobile/Light Truck - Heating and Air Conditioning (A7)	
Automobile/Light Truck - Light Vehicle Diesel Engines (A9)	
Automobile/Light Truck - Manual Drive Train and Axles (A3)	
Automobile/Light Truck - Suspension and Steering (A4)	
Medium/Heavy Truck - Brakes (T4)	
Medium/Heavy Truck - Diesel Engines (T2)	
Medium/Heavy Truck - Drive Train (T3)	
Medium/Heavy Truck - Electrical/Electronic Systems (T6)	
National Institute for Automotive Service Excellence (ASE)	
Medium/Heavy Truck - Gasoline Engines (T1)	
Medium/Heavy Truck - Heating, Ventilation and Air Conditioning (HVAC) (T7)	
Medium/Heavy Truck - Preventive Maintenance Inspection (PMI) (T8)	
Medium/Heavy Truck - Suspension and Steering (T5)	
Aviation maintenance specialist (AMS)	National Aviation Academy
Aviation maintenance engineer (AME)	

Figure 3.12 | Navy COOL Maintenance Certification Information

capability. Figure 3.13 below describes the maintenance certification information available from the Marine Corps COOL website for Marine MOS 0411, Maintenance Management Specialist.

Also remember that funds for training and testing reimbursement are available to you after you leave the service from the Veterans Administration and GI Bill. Regardless, take advantage of every opportunity for education as soon as you can, prior to leaving the service if possible.

MARINE CORPS COOL - Maintenance Certification	Certifying Body
Certified Hazardous Materials Practitioner (CHMP)	Institute of Hazardous Materials Management (IHMM)
Certified Logistics Technician (CLT (AE)	Manufacturing Skill Standards Council (MSSC)
Certified Maintenance and Reliability Technician (CMRT)	Society for Maintenance and Reliability Professionals (SMRP)
Certified Professional in Training	Institute of Packaging Professionals (IoPP)
Certified Quality Improvement Associate (CQIA)	American Society for Quality (ASQ)
CompTIA Project+	Computing Technology Industry Association (CompTIA)
Global Logistics Associate (GLA)	American Society of Transportation and Logistics, Inc. (AST&L)
ISO 9001 Foundation - Quality Certification	Professional Evaluation and Certification Board (PECB)

Figure 3.13 | Marine Corps COOL Maintenance Certification Information

Logistics Management

There are many ways to enter into the logistics management career field. Some will enter into commercial logistics management directly from college. Others will work their way up from ever increasing responsibility; simultaneously gaining education and certification. However, you will need to document the right blend of skills, experience, education and certification on your resume; thereby translating your capabilities for the hiring official, in terms that they understand. You also need to know your expected entry point into the commercial logistics arena, based upon your experience. Figure 3.14 below roughly outlines the number of years' experience generally obtained for various positions or titles held in the logistics industry. Next to this column, is a rough alignment expected entry points based upon military grade at time of departure from the service. It is important to understand that the titles do vary greatly between companies and organizations and that the chart is a generalized representation.

In a report on career success, APICS, a professional association for supply chain and operations management, stated that there is no singular easy path for career advancement within logistics management. Professionals surveyed stated that most career advancement and success came through a combination of education, certification, and work experience. Not surprisingly, dedication to career goals, mobility and hard work, lead to advancement. While there is no set linear path or place in the supply chain for each job title, many professionals shifted

Title	Years in Industry	Military Grade Entrance
Chief Operating Officer	20+	O6+
Vice President of Operations	15-20	O6
Director of Operations	10-15	O5
Manager of Operations	5-10	O4
Operations Supervisor	3-5	E7-E8, O3
Specialist	0-3	E5-E7, O1-O3

Figure 3.14 | Logistic Industry Entry Points for Military Managers

upward throughout the supply chain as their careers progressed; demonstrating the importance of knowledge and competencies throughout end-to-end supply chain management. APICS believes the statistics show that one way to accomplish this is through education and certification. On an APICS website, the organization stated recently, "While there is not a set path for operations management professionals, defining career goals; and obtaining training, education, and certifications are important milestones that help accelerate any career path."[15]

In a recent article on *5 Ways to Make Your Supply Chain & Logistics Career Journey a Smoother Climb*, the following observations are presented in Figure 3.15, which are relevant across many industries.[16]

5 Ways to Make Your Supply Chain & Logistics Career Journey a Smoother Climb	
Know the company culture	Take time to find out who are the key players are in your enterprise
Performance is important - but keep it in perspective	Find ways to be creative, through mentoring, solving problems, and identifying improvements, but don't be a spring butt
Pay attention to image	Recognize the importance of personal brand
Have a plan/share the plan	Insure the right people in the organization are aware of your ambitions and mobility desires
Network	Spread your net wide; who knows from where the next job opportunity will come

Figure 3.15 | Smooth Climb

Logistics Management Career Path

Supply Chain Digests suggest there is no better career path right now than supply chain, with the possible exception of a fracking engineer. In fact, some are calling a graduate degree in supply chain management "the new MBA".[17] The Wall Street Journal has stated that the "hot new M.B.A. is in Supply-Chain Management, where schools are ramping up their programs, adding majors and concentrations as employer demand grows".[18] So there are multiple career paths to becoming a professional logistician in this exciting and lucrative career field. Education and certification are expected as

Current Supply Chain Trends:

supplychainopz.com/ 2015/03/supply-chain-trends

professional logistician. However, your military experience may enable you to insert yourself higher into the career progression, if you can relay your experiences correctly to Human Resource department on your resume and the hiring official. The following section provides a listing of professional logistics positions that may well suit you. It is important that you understand how each position functions within the commercial arena, as there are slight nuances and variations. Some are analogous to your military experience and the positions you may have held, but there are subtle differences. There is no definitive career path in the logistics and supply chain management fields. Instead, progression requires flexibility, education, experience and certification. However you will probably need to be a distribution, logistics or IT logistics manager, before becoming a director. With this understanding, a sample career ladder is given in Figure 3.16, with light occupational descriptions following.

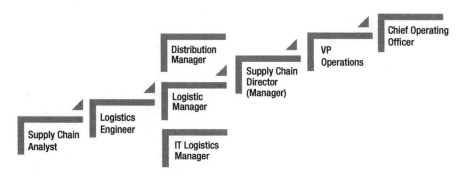

Figure 3.16 | Logistics Management Sample Career Ladder

Supply Chain Analyst

Also known as a supply chain coordinator, supply chain analysts are responsible for monitoring, analyzing, and improving supply chain processes. They predict how logistics will work, oversee operations, and then make recommendation for improved functionality. Most supply chain analysts work for logistics services providers or manufacturers.

Logistics Engineer

The logistics engineer directs, coordinates and provides subcontractors, management, and customers with logistics technology that ensures effective and economical support for manufacturing or servicing of products, systems, or equipment. They analyze contractual commitments, customer specifications, design changes, and other data to plan and develop logistic program activities from conceptual stage through life-cycle of product. He/she resolves problems in area of logistics to ensure meeting of contractual commitments. Additionally, they develop and initiate preparation of handbooks, bulletins, and information systems to provide logistics support. The logistics engineer compiles data on standardization and interoperability of parts to expedite logistics activities. Another critical function is the determination of logistic support sequences, time phasing and problem resolution while considering such areas as environmental and human factors affecting employees.

Logistic Manager

Distribution to customers of the finished products is the number one concern of the logistic manager. He or she defines, manages and controls the work of haulers/transporters in order to provide the customer with the expected level of service and minimize stocks. He also guarantees the procurement of finished products from factories.[19] They analyze and coordinate the company's supply chain, while managing nearly every aspect of the chain, including procurement of the product, distribution, allocation, and delivery.

Distribution Manager

The Distribution Manager defines the distribution network according to service and costs objectives, and assists in defining transportation modes to suppliers.

He develops benchmarking analysis on the market, and defines and develops optimization processes with the aim to maximize efficiency and continuous service improvement.[20]

IT Logistics Manager

Logistics automation or the IT logistics manager is responsible for the application of computer software and/or automated machinery to improve the efficiency of logistics operations. Typically this refers to operations within a warehouse or distribution center, with broader tasks undertaken by supply chain management systems and enterprise resource planning systems.

This deals in everything from bar code or radio-frequency identification (RFID) technologies to the processing systems that use the associated data.

Supply Chain Director (Manager)

The supply chain director promotes the development of logistics management as a core competence for the organization, enabling the sector's supply chains to service dynamic customer requirements at optimum costs. They define and manage the logistics budget (logistics costs); contribute to define and realize company strategy while supporting vice president (VP) or chief operating officer (COO) on logistic issues. They promote corporate logistical innovation, lead projects and improvement activities while ensuring the correct production planning, integration, distribution, production allocation and customer service in terms of product availability and delivery.[21]

Logistics Management Certifications

As a professional military logistician, you have the experience and the talent, but you may not have the documentation and resume necessary to compete commercially. Professional certifications are prevalent in the logistics career filed. To increase your competitive advantage, you may very well desire to gain a certification in logistics prior to departing the service.

There are a multitude of certifications within the logistics management career field and each one requires familiarity with the certifying organization, self-study and then formalized testing. Appendix B provides a listing of certification organizations and their associated web addresses. The APICS survey discussed earlier also drove home the importance of logistics certification. Seventy percent of senior professionals believe training and certification, followed closely by networking, are the most important methods for career development in the logistics management field. Forty percent have obtained some form of logistics management certification. Important to note, most logistics professionals certify after being in the profession for at least five years, while logisticians at the managerial level, hold certification.[22]

So what does all this mean to you? As the *Transitioning Military Logistician*, obtain a commercial logistics management certification early in your transition from the military. This will give you a competitive advantage, and it will be expected for many logistic management positions. Once on the job site, you will find some of your contemporaries will have taken the time and effort to certify, and you will have the quiet confidence to know that you are capable and competitive.

Figure 3.17 below is a sampling of the certifications and their associated credentialing body. These are available to you as you transition into commercial logistics management.

Logistics Management Certification	Credentialing Body
Certified Logistics Technician (CLTAE)	Manufacturing Skills Standards Council
Certified Production Technician (CPT)	
Certified in Transportation and Logistics (CTL)	American Society of Transportation and Logistics, Inc. (AST&L)
Certified Master Logistician (CML)	The International Society of Logistics (SOLE)
Certified Professional Logistician (CPL)	
Demonstrated Logistician	
Distinguished Logistics Professional (DLP)	American Society of Transportation and Logistics, Inc. (AST&L)
Global Logistics Associate (GLA)	
Professional Designation in Logistics and Supply Chain Management (PLS)	
APICS Certified in Production and Inventory Management (CPIM)	APICS The Association for Operations
APICS Certified Supply Chain Professional (CSCP)	
APICS Supply Chain Operations Reference Professional (SCOR-P)	
Certified Fellow in Production and Inventory Management (CFPIM)	

Figure 3.17 | Logistics Management Sample Career Ladder

Government Certification

For those desiring to stay in the logistics career field as a civil servant, often the DAU certification process is an appropriate method for job security and promotion. Remember, anyone in the acquisition career field can take the training, but only civil servants and active duty military can get the certification. The Defense Acquisition Workforce Improvement Act (DAWIA) required the Department of Defense (DoD) to establish a process through which persons in the acquisition workforce would be recognized as having achieved professional status. Certification is the procedure through which a military service or DoD Component determines that an employee meets the education, training, and experience standards required for a career level in any acquisition, technology, and logistics career field."[23]

DAU Courses:
dau.mil/default.aspx

Certifications are only available for DoD civilian employees, military and civilians assigned to an acquisition coded position and select military officers whose career development will include assignment to acquisition-coded positions. Even though certification is not a qualification requirement for employment within the DoD, job announcements will view this certification as a "quality ranking factor" not a "qualification factor". Therefore, all DoD personnel filling acquisition positions have 24 months to achieve the certification standards (career field/path and level) assigned to the position.

In addition to the Level I, II and III, career field guides are given on the DAU site for the most current career field certification standards required of the Defense Acquisition Workforce in accordance with the acquisition position. As of the date of this book's publication, Figure 3.18 shows the career field certifications currently available through DAU.[24]

For example, if you want to pursue Life Cycle Logistics positions and are required to obtain a DAU certification, you would need to qualify at Level I, II, or III, depending on your position. You do not necessarily have to qualify at each level in order, but Level III would require prerequisites from the lower level certifications. Each requirement for each Acquisition Career Field is specified

DAU CAREER FIELD CERTIFICATION FUNCTIONAL AREAS

Auditing	Information Technology
Business – Cost Estimating	**Life Cycle Logistics**
Business – Financial Management	Program Management
Contracting	Production, Quality and Manufacturing
Engineering	Purchasing
Facilities Engineering	Science and Technology Manager
Industrial/Contract Property Management	Test and Evaluation

Figure 3.18 | DAU Career Field Certification Functional Areas

at the DAU website. By way of example, Figure 3.19 shows the requirements for DAWIA certification of Level I in the logistics management career field:

DAU LOGISTICS CORE CERTIFICATION STANDARDS

Acquisition Training	ACQ 101 Fundamentals of Systems Acquisition Management ENG 101 Fundamentals of Systems Engineering
Functional Training	LOG 101 Acquisition Logistics Fundamentals LOG 102 Fundamentals of System Sustainment Management' LOG 103 Reliability, Availability, and Maintainability (RAM) CLL 008 Designing for Supportability in DoD Systems CLL 011 Performance Based Logistics (PBL)
Education	Formal education not required for certification
Experience	1 year of life cycle logistics experience in an acquisition and/or sustainment organization

Figure 3.19 | *DAU* Logistics Core Certification Standards

The silver lining for government certification is two-fold. First, this is high quality, government specific, on-line training that is available to you. Second, this training is available free of charge. If you go the civil service route, this training is absolutely essential and will propel your career and significantly enhance your knowledge and skills. Additionally, there are additional certifications available at the Air Force Institute of Technology (AFIT) in Supply Chain Management Certificate Program. The National Defense University offers a directory of joint courses available at the Center for Joint and Strategic Logistics.

The Army Logistics University also offers numerous course works for Department of the Army (DA) civil servants. Generally, this education and training will need to be taken as a government employee. If possible, take this training prior to your departure from the service.

NDU Courses:
cjsl.ndu.edu/Resources.aspx

Education Options

As mentioned earlier, most logistics managers will have Bachelor's Degrees. If you have not obtained a degree but are considering the logistics management career field, consider getting the degree in one of the courses of study listed below in Figure 3.20. Colleges and universities throughout the country offer the following Associates, Bachelors and Masters Degrees.

DEGREE FIELD OF STUDY
Logistics
Logistics and Supply Chain Management
Logistics management degree
Transportation and Logistics
Humanitarian Supply Chain Management
Logistics Management (Economics)
Econometrics and Operations Research
Logistics in Commerce
Operations and Information Management
Logistics Information Systems

Figure 3.20 | Logistics Management Degree Opportunities

There are many veteran friendly colleges and universities. Syracuse University is one such university offering a Master's of Science degree in Logistical Technology (LogTech).

Make sure to use your Army and Navy E-learning benefit prior to getting out. A multitude of courses in management exist on this site. Procurement and vendor management are available in the operations

Syracuse University Info:
whitman.syr.edu/programs-and-academics/programs/executive-defense/defense-programs/logtech-ms-scm/

management track. This tremendous benefit, leading to many certifications and degrees, goes away upon your departure from the service. Many of these credits are approved by the American Council on Education (ACE).[25]

**Army e-Learning
Course Catalog:**
atrrs.army.mil/
selfdevctr/sfcatalog.pdf

Other Training Options

What if you are tired of logistics? If you are ready to move on from logistics and desire other training, but have not yet exited the service, know that there is currently free training available through the Veterans Career Transition Program (VCTP), provided by Syracuse University and JPMorgan Chase, Inc. These have specified and independent study learning paths with up to six months free online training via Microsoft, Oracle, CISCO and the Project Management Institute, leading to certification. Additionally, GR8MilitaryLog.com has other superb books leading to additional great career fields.

VCTP Information
vets.syr.edu/employment/
vctp-certification-paths

Assessment #4 *(Skills)*

Figure 3.21 is the fourth assessment in the book and explores your personal preparedness for the logistics career field. You may answers the questions here. When you are ready to analyze them, refer to Chapter 5. You can also use the companion guide to this book, available for download at Gr8MilitaryLog.com. Read each question and choose the correct answer for your current situation.

4: SKILLS	Strongly Disagree	Disagree	Neither Agree OR Disagree	Agree	Strongly Agree
I enjoy working in the logistics career field.					
I have pursued an certification or degree in commercial logistics.					
I have performed logistics functions or tasks in the past.					
I have worked with repair parts, supplies, vehicle maintenance or moved materiel.					
I have created training schedules or plans in the military.					
I have reviewed different types of Logistics certifications and analyzed the best certification for my situation.					
I enjoy leading groups and organizations.					
I have planned logistics operations in the military.					
I feel confident in my understanding of commercial logistics operations.					
I desire to get a CDL or certification in maintenance, supply or logistics management prior to leaving the service.					

Figure 3.21 | Skills Assessment

Summary

Once comfortable with commercial logistics, logistics management concepts, career ladder, associated certifications and training, you will have a competitive advantage when transitioning from the military into the logistics career field. The choice to prepare yourself to meet and excel in your new career and enjoy the career benefits is yours to make. We encourage you to continue your education and learn all you can about logistics as a profession and to gain an awareness that transcends job titles, careers and industries. As the story indicates below, many have come before you and have transitioned into the exciting career field of logistics; and you will too. The real-world, best practice tools and techniques that you successfully will use to provide logistics management will be recognized for many years to come.

Dave Buchanan
Remain Flexible and Calm

AFTER GRADUATING FROM HIGH SCHOOL IN WILLIAMSBURG, VIRGINIA WITH A GREAT HIGH SCHOOL BASKETBALL CAREER, DAVE BUCHANAN QUICKLY LEARNED THAT HE WAS CHASING A DREAM. After trying this endeavor, Dave worked hard, landed a ROTC scholarship, and hit the books.

After graduating, Dave's was selected to the Army Quartermaster Corps. He talked to others and quickly understood that logistics made the world move forward. Dave also began to realize that being in the logistics field could become a key element of success for both his military career and successful businesses career later in the civilian sector.

After his initial training, Dave moved to Germany, where he took over management of a general support warehouse with over 17,000 line items for the V Mechanized Corps. With V Corps, he gained a true sense of belonging, as the work led to the successful support of Desert Shield/Desert Storm. Dave's culminating assignment was as a Forward Support Company Commander for the 3rd Infantry Division in Fort Stewart, Georgia.

Dave made a deliberate decision to transition his career towards the commercial sector. With little available in the form of a transition assistance program, Dave relied on his own limited research and others who had come before him, creating a resume and utilizing his transferable logistical skills. He landed his first commercial logistics position as a driver manager in a refrigerated trucking company in Wisconsin. Dave found that this was the closest he would come to replicating the logistics operations world of the Army, loving the daily problem solving and the realization that every problem presented a new challenge. Not long thereafter, Dave found himself working toward more interesting commercial logistics positions. He moved to Third

79

Party Logistics (3PL) and became an account manager. Later, as a director of logistics he found this experience, coupled with his previous military and civilian positions with diverse customers and supply chains to be instrumental. His military leadership training and experience consistently propelled him toward complex supply chain and commercial logistics leadership roles. Dave has worked in leadership roles for third party logistics providers, warehouse operations, and asset based transportation companies, while eventually attaining the level of Director of Operations. Today, after almost 30 years in the logistics field in and out of the military, Dave continues to provide logistics management for clients and customers in a consulting role. Reflecting on many of the skills that he learned early on as an Army logistician, Dave believes one must remain flexible, calm in crisis situations, and focus on being valuable to the operation. Dave remains proud that he has been able to provide that value for the military, civilian companies and to the customers of both.

4

Understanding the Market Place

TREMENDOUS OPPORTUNITIES ABOUND IN THE COMMERCIAL AND PUBLIC SECTORS. The challenge is understanding and making an informed decision about where to conduct your job search. This very important decision needs to incorporate your comfort levels with risk, job satisfaction, security and growth. Learning about your desires as they relate to market place characteristics, will give you a distinct advantage in your job search decision. You may have already settled on a target job market. However, if you are unsure, look to this chapter to provide you with the tools to evaluate the pros and cons of your target market place.

Some transitioning personnel believe they will step into a great paying and interesting job for the rest of their life, immediately after leaving the service. However, this is not typical. Most of us change jobs, companies, and career fields many times. Learning the advantages and disadvantages of multiple transitions can better prepare you and your family.

Opportunities after the military service fall into roughly four sectors. Three of these sectors are the

> **"Opportunities multiply as they are seized."**
>
> Sun Tzu 孫子
> *The Art of War*

81

focus of this chapter; civil service, government contracting, and commercial market place. For those that enjoy risk and working independently, entrepreneurship is a forth option. There is a wealth of knowledge readily available on the entrepreneurship market. Entrepreneurship is not a focus as it is beyond the scope and objective of this book.

Each market place is explored with regard to environment, opportunity, pay, benefits and career path as they relate to your interest and desires. Options and insights are offered so that you can weigh and consider all facets that impact you the most, from work/life balance to job benefits.

After looking at each sector, the market places are compared within the framework described above. A marketplace assessment is presented to further assist in identifying key factors while determining the best fit for you and your next position. As you read this chapter, note that the terms public sector, government, and civil service are all used interchangeably. Likewise, private sector, commercial company, and corporation are terms used in lieu of commercial market place. DoD Contracting is considered a hybrid to these distinct sectors.

Civil Service Market Place

The federal government is the largest employment sector in the nation, hiring nearly 300,000 new employees every year. There are many government departments and agencies. All have many differences, from culture, professional opportunity, and employee satisfaction, and in some cases, pay scales.[1] Generally, civil service provides a tremendous opportunity for those desiring a stable work environment, great benefits and good pay. The reality is that people do not take civil service positions to get wealthy. In general, government workers want to use their skills and make a difference. Therefore, many choose civil service for these reasons, along with a growing number of transitioning military.

"Most candidates interested in working for the government fully understand three clear benefits," said Evan Lesser, co-founder and director of

Federal benefits:

usa.gov/Federal
Employees/Benefits.shtml

ClearanceJobs.com, a secure website designed to match security-cleared job candidates with top defense industry employers. "First, is the issue of job security. Compared to contractors, Federal agencies are less subject to budget funding shortfalls and cancelled or re-bid contracts. Second, job seekers see a more structured promotion ladder. And third, working for the nation's largest employer means excellent health and retirement benefits."[2] If you are unaware, workers in commercial firms are three times more likely to be fired, compared to federal employees. Civil service positions are generally more stable. This is comforting if stability is one of your most compelling decision factors.

Environment

The Partnership for Public Service (PPS), in concert with the audit and financial professional services firm Deloitte, annually publishes the "The Best Places to Work in the Federal Government". This cross agency assessment provides civil servants' opinions on workplace issues ranging from leadership, work-life balance, pay and personal ability for innovation.

John Palguta, PPS Vice President of Policy, stated "The reason people go to work for the government is because they want to do something meaningful and make a difference. Civil servants want to make good use of their skills and be engaged in mission accomplishment." The PPS assessment demonstrates civil servant personal job satisfaction and overall organization satisfaction.[3] An important factor making up organization satisfaction is pay. The last couple of years have been difficult for civil servant salary increases. Not surprisingly, recent reports show a significant categorical drop in satisfaction of federal pay, due to the political and economic environment. Potentially due to fiscal concerns, there was also a decline in training and development opportunities, and rewards and advancement.[4]

Federal workplace survey:
Bestplacestowork.org/BPTW/rankings/governmentwide

Additionally, assessment results are broken into federal agency size categories. Not surprisingly, the Departments of Navy, Air Force and Army are all listed and considered large agencies with 15,000 or more employees. Interestingly, for the civil servants interviewed, National Aeronautics and Space Administration finished on top with the highest satisfaction, and the Department of Homeland Security finished last. Figure 4.1 provides statistical results in overall job satisfaction for all federal large agencies. No sector receives a perfect score of 100, but the higher the score, indicates greater personal job satisfaction within that agency.

RANK	LARGE AGENCY (15,000 OR MORE EMPLOYEES)	SCORE
1	National Aeronautics and Space Administration	74
2	Department of Commerce	67.6
3	Intelligence Community	67.3
4	Department of State	65.6
5	Department of Justice	63.58
6	Social Security Administration	63
7	Department of Health and Human Services	61.9
8	Department of Transportation	60.9
9	Department of the Treasury	59.5
10	Environmental Protection Agency (tie)	59.3
10	Department of the Navy (tie)	59.3
12	Department of the Interior	58.9
13	Department of Veterans Affairs	57.3
14	Department of the Air Force	57.2
15	Office of the Secretary of Defense, Joint Staff, Defense Agencies	57
16	Department of Agriculture	56.1
17	Department of Labor (tie)	55.6
17	Department of the Army (tie)	55.6
19	Department of Homeland Security	46.8

Figure 4.1 | Statistical Results for Job Satisfaction – Large Agency

Opportunity

Generally, civil service positions provide tremendous opportunities for military members in transition. The federal government gives you an advantage due to your veteran status. Having served in a war, having a military connected disability or having served on active duty all give you an advantage and put you in different competitive categories. Therefore, your military service provides a significant benefit when competing for high quality civil-service positions.

When applying for civil service positions, you need to understand how the job announcement enables or precludes your advantageous veteran status. In many civil service applications, veteran status is awarded extra 'points' when identified by the applicant. You may be eligible to compete under one or more categories designed for veterans such as Veterans' Recruitment Appointment

Civil Service Job Site:
USAJOBS.GOV

(VRA), 30 Percent or More Disabled Veterans, and Veterans Employment Opportunities Act of 1998 (VEOA). These special hiring authorities for veterans give you a significant advantage if you are qualified. Figure 4.2 below summarizes these hiring authorities:

AUTHORITY	PROVISION	WHO IT APPLIES TO
VRA	VRA allows appointment of eligible Veterans up to the GS-11 or equivalent grade level.	• Disabled Veterans • Veterans who served on active duty in the Armed Forces during a war declared by Congress, or in a campaign or expedition for which a campaign badge has been authorized. • Veterans who, while serving on active duty in the Armed Forces, participated in a military operation for which the Armed Forces Service Medal (AFSM) was awarded • Veterans separated from active duty within the past 3 years.
30% Disabled	Enables a hiring manager to appoint an eligible candidate to any position for which he or she is qualified, without competition. Unlike the VRA, there is no grade-level limitation.	• Disabled Veterans who were retired from active military service with a service-connected disability rating of 30 percent or more • Disabled Veterans rated by the Department of Veterans Affairs (VA) as having a compensable service-connected disability of 30 percent or more.
VEOA	• Gives preference eligible and certain eligible Veterans' access to jobs that otherwise only would have been available to status employees.	• Preference eligible • Service personnel separated after 3 or more years of continuous active service performed under honorable conditions.

Figure 4.2 | Civil Service Hiring Authorities for Veterans

Remember, your competition when applying for these positions are current federal employees with status and other United States citizens. Therefore, understanding your veteran eligibility is critical. Also, be aware that your eligibility does not make you qualified for the position. You may be eligible under a special hiring authority, but you may not be qualified based on your experience or education.

Veterans transitioning to civil service:
fedshirevets.gov/hire/hm/shav

The difference between eligibility and qualifications can be summed up as follows. Qualification is based solely on your knowledge, skills, and abilities (KSA's), and education, as discussed in chapters two and three. Eligibility is meeting one or more criteria such as disabled veteran. A recent dimension in determining qualification for a job is the use of self-assessments, which are now becoming more of a standard than the exception. A series of questions are asked of the candidate during the application process to determine if you meet the KSAs for the position. Civil service hiring is also based on your capability to demonstrate your experience at the next lower level. So, if you are applying for a GS 12, your resume and questionnaire answers need to demonstrate your competencies and experience at the GS 11 level. Therefore, if you do not demonstrate your qualification for the position, your documentation will not be forwarded to the hiring official for review. Further information on answering federal self-assessments can be found on monster.com.

Like other market places, there are significant advantages when it comes to mobility or being able to move to serve the needs of the government. When finding a position in a different locality you may receive pay for a move much like that in the military. Every position on USAJOBS.GOV will tell you if relocation is authorized. Sometimes, the department will offer relocation if it is hard to find someone with certain qualifications and/or interest in going to that particular location. For example, finding a job with relocation to the

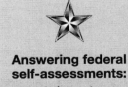

Answering federal self-assessments:
govcentral.monster.com/benefits/articles/2370-best-ways-to-answer-federal-self-assessments

Washington D.C. area can be difficult. However, most rural locations without a significant local applicant pool will often provide relocation and/or financial incentive.

The best method for applying for civil service positions is through the comprehensive website "USAJOBS.GOV". This website not only posts jobs available by title description and location, it allows you to apply and track your application status. Helpful resume and application tips are given, enabling you to put your best foot forward.

Pay

Pay is a subject that is of great interest to all of us. Government Service (GS) pay scales operate on grade levels and geography. GS pay tables are standardized much like military pay tables, with the addition of locality pay adjustments. In 2014, a GS-14 Supply Chain Manager in San Francisco can earn an annual salary of $115,613 to $150,291 depending on step. While in Tampa, the same position pays from $97,657 to $126,249. Entry level GS-12s Intermodal Dispatcher can earn $69,497 in Salt Lake City, and about $6,000 a year more in the Washington D.C. area. Therefore, you have to look at the correct scale for the location for which you are applying. As an example, Tampa has no special "locality pay area" table. In the case where there is no scale for the metropolitan area you are considering, look at the scale called "Rest of United States". Figure 4.3 below delineates the GS Pay Scale for the San Francisco (35.5% locality payment) area. Remember, no locality pay is given in overseas areas. Instead, overseas employees receive cost of living allowances (COLA).

GS PAY Tables:
opm.gov/policy-data-
oversight/pay-leave/salaries
wages/2014/general-schedule

Benefits

A tremendous number of benefits are available to civil servants. Benefits are organized into five major categories: benefits and insurance, leave and work-

Grade	Step 1	Step 2	Step 3	Step 4	Step 5	Ste
1	$ 24,301	$ 25,114	$ 25,922	$ 26,726	$ 27,534	$ 28
2	27,323	27,973	28,878	29,644	29,975	30
3	29,811	30,805	31,798	32,791	33,785	3
4	33,467	34,582	35,697	36,812	37,927	39,0
5	37,443	38,692	39,941	41,190	42,438	43,
6	41,738	43,129	44,520	45,910	47,301	

SALARY TABLE 20
INCORPORATING THE 1% GENERAL SCHEDULE INCRE
FOR THE LOCALITY PAY AREA OF SAN JOSE-S
TOTAL INCREASE
EFFECTIVE JANUA

Annual Rates by Grade

Figure 4.3 | Salary Table 2014-SF, Locality Pay for San Francisco

life balance, pay and savings, retirement, and personnel records. There is some variety between agencies, and the country's economy plays a great role in the availability of some benefits such as education. The major benefit categories are listed in Figure 4.4, but there are many benefits in each category. A complete detailed list is available at each agency website and at www.usa.gov/Federal-Employees/Benefits.shtml. Remember, not all benefits are available from each department or agency.

Civil Service Benefits:
usa.gov/Federal-Employees/Benefits.shtml

HIGH LEVEL BENEFITS FOR CIVIL SERVANTS
- Benefits and Insurance Programs
- Leave and Work-Life Balance
- Pay and Savings Plans
- Retirement
- Personnel Records

Figure 4.4 | Civil Service Benefits[5]

DoD Contracting Market Place

Many believe that the DoD contracting life blends the best of both attributes of GS and commercial market place while staying in a career supporting the military. The DoD contract environment is different from your military experience. You are still ultimately working for the defense of the nation, but you serve two masters. More importantly, the risk and rewards are both potentially greater than that of the civil service.

As a DoD contractor, you remain engaged with the defense of our nation. Many service members want to spend their post-military career doing something that feels familiar, and comfortable. This is why many pursue DoD contracting after military service. Transitioning to a DoD contracting position gives you comfort of a familiar language, and a grasp on the needs of the mission and organization.[6]

Environment

For many, DoD contracting is a very appealing post military career. In addition to potentially better wages for your work efforts than civil service, you have the potential to stay within the same department or agency you already know and understand, while receiving significant flexibility not previously enjoyed. In most locations, you have the right to move on to another position or company should you become weary of your contract situation, bosses attitude, or government leadership. This knowledge and understanding provides relief for many in difficult or challenging situations.

Understanding the associated risks of DoD contracting is also very important. First, some find the government-contractor relationship challenging, especially after having been on the government side for a long period. If you choose to remain in the DoD environment, never lose site of the fact that the contractual relationship is adversarial by its very nature. There is goodness in this adversarial relationship. It is not only good for the taxpayer, but also provides constant checks and balances for both sides. The desire is to have a harmonious environment, with equilibrium between government over-watch and contract performance. If either side gains the upper hand, then a difficult and challenging work environment will exist.

"One of the most important but difficult tasks in contract administration is to develop a proper working relationship. Cooperation

between the parties is essential if the work is to be successfully per-
formed, and yet the parties are, in a very real sense, adversaries.
The Government often attempts to obtain performance within the
contract price, while the contractor attempts to maximize profits
either by doing the minimum acceptable work or by attempting to
obtain price increase."[7]

Why is this information important to you? Understanding the contract and government relationship is essential to your day-to-day life as a contractor. The question you face is how to deal with these types of relationship issues. Do you enjoy working through these types of challenges with contract leaders, program managers, and associated government counterparts? It is important to find the right fit. Learning to understand the challenges that lie ahead and being prepared to identify them, process them, and create optional courses of action will help you be successful. Examples of challenges you will face as a DoD contractor are summarized below.

One of the first things you will have to reconcile as a new contractor is that most contracts have an estimated date for completion. This proves challenging for most former military folks as your term of service was relatively guaranteed. How to deal with uncertainty of follow on work with your contract can be challenging and stressful. This is potentially the contractor's greatest anxiety. Not only does the contractor have to perform well, satisfy the customer, accomplish the tasks on time and to standard, but he or she must be keenly aware of the remaining contract duration and how well the contract at large is performing.

Recruit Military:
Connecting organizations
with veterans.
recruitmilitary.com

If you desire a steady income, you may find coping with this risk difficult. The contractors that feel most comfortable with this arrangement will typically grow a sizable rainy day fund (2-3 months' salary) to assist during contract transitional periods. This risk mitigation strategy will provide some peace of mind, especially in these challenging economic and ever changing political times. Always remember, that even in a down economy, the government remains the largest single employer in the country and there are plenty of contracting jobs available, especially if you are willing to relocate.

Another challenge to reconcile with is that you will be working with either a military or a civil servant government lead. They will have the final say on decisions. Constrained by rules and regulations, the federal government is not famous for innovation or speed of bureaucratic consensus. These challenges may feel stifling or even frustrate some into choosing to move on to another occupation.

Opportunity

Like civil service, federal contractors receive similar benefits with regard to mobility, future work and security. Contracts extend well beyond Washington D.C., with departments, agencies and offices around the world. That makes finding a job for those seeking a specific location, or desiring an opportunity to change localities, a great potential benefit. If you are mobile and good at what you do, the contract industry is going to have a job for you.[8] People move from job to job as contracts come and go. A DoD contracting career offers a significant chance for mobility and professional growth.[9]

Professional diversity is an added benefit of being a DoD contractor. As you acquire a variety of experience, you will be increasingly sought after. You will have a chance to move in and out of various professional experiences. If you are already an expert in one area, working different tasks and functions means you will have the chance to develop new skills and explore potential new specialized areas.

Finally, like civil service, your security clearance is invaluable if you choose to stay in DoD contracting. If your clearance re-investigation date has passed and you have lost your clearance, but you have the experience needed, many contractors will offer to recapture your clearance as part of your hiring package. Additionally, many federal contractors will offer 'upgrades' of your clearance for required positions to meet certain contract requirements. You will not necessarily be reminded of your periodic investigation dates, so stay on top of your clearance. If a life event occurs such as financial issues, divorce, or arrest, make sure you inform your security officer quickly.

Job availability, good starting salaries and promotion potential are all positive aspects of contracting as long as you can go to where the jobs are. A defense contracting career is often the preference of many. If you have the skills wanted by the contractor at the right time, they will hire you on the spot with minimal paperwork and put you to work immediately. Further, you will have more control of your own destiny as your performance is the driving force in your career path. If you are performing, you will be promoted. If you are dissatisfied, then move to a more demanding job opportunity offering better pay.

Pay

As a contractor, you have a greater ability to nego-tiate a salary than your civil servant counter parts. As a company competes for new work with the government, a proposal is developed outlining various positions on the contract. The company will bid a specified price that takes into account a pay band for each position. Once awarded, the program manager has some flexibility within the

Negotiating Salary:
See Appendix D or go to:
GR8MilitaryLog.com

pay band when hiring employees. This information may allow you to negotiate salary within the pay band for your desired position. Therefore, you will have to request a salary within a position's pay band, or you will probably not be hired.

As in the earlier quote from Sun Tzu, it is obvious the greatest road to success is to know yourself and know your environment. It is often said the first party to mention a figure during salary negotiation will not fare as well in the nego-tiation. Therefore, when questioned about your salary requirements, it is best to ask about the pay band for your position and request a well thought out number that resides within that pay band. Appendix D of this book provides a method for determining a realistic salary request.

Benefits

First, know that human resource organizations will have specialists and experts that will explain and share current offerings in line with federal and state laws. Generally, there is minimal variation between contract companies when it comes to benefit packages. Regardless of which federal contractor you work for, you will find 100-150 hours offered as Paid Time Off (PTO) annually; or stated in military terms, leave. Of interest is that you accrue and take PTO by the hour and not by the day. This is helpful as you will need to take PTO occasionally for doctors' appointments, sick leave, or vacation. Unfortunately, most of the appointments that you are used to going to during a military duty day will have to be charged as PTO. Another option, if available, is flex time. Many companies desire that you get 40 hours of work in one week or 80 hours over a two-week period. Often, you can flex hours within the pay period so that you could work 42 hours one week and 38 the next. This type of arrangement varies by company. Regardless, just remember that the time cards are archived for inspection by the Defense Contract Audit Agency (DCAA). Therefore, contract and personal integrity are on the line and the time card must accurately reflect hours worked.

With regards to health benefits, most companies offer comprehensive healthcare where you pay a share and the company pays a share. If you are a retiree, some companies adjust your salary if you utilize your retiree healthcare benefit. Just know, if you desire to use a company's healthcare you can, but there will more than likely be a deduction from your pay check for the benefit. Vision and dental are shared benefits as well. Just like your health insurance, if you are using TRICARE as an example, this benefit may not be of interest to you.

A flexible spending account is often available by larger companies in which you place some of your salary into an account for healthcare related expenditures. The dollars you place in this program reduce your taxable income, but must all be used for healthcare by the end of each year. Most companies, big and small will offer a 401(k) plan for long-term retirement savings. These plans will generally be matching funds up to about 3-5%. The company will determine which investment group you will be buying into and you will generally have a choice of funds. Some companies allow all your dollars to be fully "vested" upon your initial investment. Others will allow you to have their matching funds after a vesting period has surpassed (i.e., 50% vested after 2 years, 100% after 3 years). These vesting periods vary considerably between companies. Just remember that the 401(k) is for long term retirement savings and significant penalties will normally be applied if you take out money prior to age 59½.[10] Additionally, some companies offer different types of stock options at discounted rates. This is an inexpensive way to invest in your company as you avoid brokerage fees in addition to any discount offered. Regardless, it is always recommended to place enough money in the 401(k) to get the matching funds, as you do not want to leave money on the table.

Larger companies have educational, training and certification assistance. Training authorization typically requires justification for the position you are in. Generally, companies will ask that you sign a document stating that you will not leave the company for some period of time (often 1 year) after taking the training dollars. This needs to be considered prior to taking training if you are thinking about changing companies, because some will hold back your last pay check to pay for your training if you have not completed the allotted time.

If you have not surmised, bigger DoD contract companies generally offer bigger and better benefits. The alternative is that smaller companies may have greater salary and might be more attractive to employees desiring fewer benefits. Therefore, if benefits are not that important and more pay is a consideration, you may consider going to work for a smaller company. For example, if you have retiree benefits, you could negotiate more in salary. Finally, some small companies have greater flexibility for profit sharing with their employees. Regardless, weigh all of the benefits, salary, profit sharing and bonus capabilities to find the total compensation of the position. This exercise will assist you in weighing your options when comparing multiple job offers.

Commercial Market Place

Transitioning into the commercial market place from the military requires considerable risk tolerance and a high level of confidence in your ability to perform in a competitive environment. As mentioned at the beginning of this chapter, workers in commercial firms are three times more likely to be fired as compared to federal employees. Working in the commercial market is not for the faint of heart, and the risks must be managed. However, most working in the commercial market quickly state that the rewards for this risk outweigh the job security of civil service.

Environment

Because workers strive for personal growth and reward, the commercial environment is often very competitive. In the commercial environment, employees generally try to remain competitive through innovation and providing business value to the organization. This determination and drive often require numerous man hours above and beyond a traditional 40 hour work week. Understandably, most workers join the commercial market place to earn significant amount of money, to be trained or gain experience, positioning themselves to earn significant money later.

It is always the desire in commercial market to achieve profitability and make money. Maximizing profit will drive all business decisions. If there are two choices, the best business case will be selected. Companies and managers will consistently pursue the highest potential profit at the best value every time they make a business decision. What this means to you as a potential worker in the commercial environment is that you must understand this concept and remain viable to the company, otherwise your services will not be needed for long. The profit concept is foreign to most public sector workers, including service members. Be advised, this concept sometimes becomes a bias against hiring veterans for some commercial hiring managers.

In high performing companies, there is tremendous focus on the bottom line. Managers desire to achieve this focus which leads to well understood, top to bottom goals and objectives. Two most important objectives driving decision making in the commercial market place are solution and price. Focusing on solution and price typically drives satisfaction and value in the commercial market. Managers must focus on providing and creating added value through the products and services offered by their company. The best solution is sought, as it increases return on investment and profit. Therefore, you need to be synchronized with management as you are held accountable for your work, and you are rewarded for success and potentially fired for failure.[11]

You need to understand what drives value in your work environment. Knowing this will help you align your day-to-day work effort as you deal with the customer as well as connect better when looking for a job. Nothing is more nerve racking than going to an interview or giving a presentation and not understanding how your employer perceives or derives value. Further, you are far better off talking to your leadership about their view regarding the best solution and profit, rather than unfinanced requirements and perceived cost savings which do not aid the organization's bottom line.

Opportunity

The commercial sector is set apart from the public sector with regard to rapid personal growth potential for achievers with financial reward and the promise of a creative and innovative environment. Rapid change is pervasive with the ever-changing business environment, and you will be rewarded if you embrace and become part of the change. One of the great attributes associated with the commercial market place is that your high performance will enable you to progress quickly without regard to a pay scale or longevity. As you work on your professional goals and career path, utilize opportunities to gain additional and diverse experience. Seek out ways to gain internal qualifications through training that aligns with your career goals. Keep in mind where you want to be and take on challenges to posture yourself for future success.

Financial reward is based largely on your ability to remain viable and valuable to the organizations. If you are adding to the bottom line you will be rewarded financially. The company rewards your positive impact and participation because if you move on, it may lose profit and key knowledge to the competition.

Innovation and creativity are also well rewarded in the private sector, as long as the innovation aids to the company's competitiveness, market position, or bottom line.

Remember, to remain competitive, companies will seek innovative workers and it will make change based on the business environment. If you like an exciting and dynamic environment, the commercial sector is for you.

Pay

Conventional wisdom has it that you'll always make more money in the commercial market place, with lower pay being the trade-off for job security in the federal government.

That's generally true. The Federal Salary Council, a group of union officials and pay policy experts, says federal workers overall earn about 35 percent less than their commercial-sector peers.[12]

Another aspect to remember is that your logistics management experience from the military, if understood by your civilian hiring manager, will assist in landing a good paying job. Figure 4.5 below gives national sample salaries for logistics workers.[13]

Figure 4.5 | National Salary Sample by Job Function

Benefits

In general, benefits are similar or better than DoD contracting. The one exception is small business as, you may have fewer benefits. That being said, small businesses must offer the following benefits as they are considered mandatory by the federal government.[14]

- Time off to vote, serve on a jury and perform military service.
- Comply with all workers' compensation requirements.

- Withhold FICA taxes from employees' paychecks and pay your own portion of FICA taxes, providing employees with retirement and disability benefits.
- Pay state and federal unemployment taxes, thus providing benefits for unemployed workers.
- Contribute to state short-term disability programs in states where such programs exist.
- Comply with the Federal Family and Medical Leave (FMLA).

Surprisingly, the following benefits are not required to be given to employees and you may see a variation of these benefits at every company.

- Retirement plans
- Health plans (most employers are still working through the the Affordable Care Act)
- Dental or vision plans
- Life insurance plans
- Paid vacations, holidays or sick leave

Having said all of this, most large companies offer tremendous benefits and some unexpected surprises upon arrival. Price Waterhouse Coopers (PWC)[15] advertises the following "Perks" on their website:

- **Sabbatical:** Employees can take four-week sabbaticals with 20 percent to 50 percent of pay.
- **Tuition Reimbursement and Scholarships:** Employees can get up to $5,250 in financial assistance to further their education.
- **401(k):** PWC contributes 5 percent of an employees' annual pay to their 401(k) retirement savings plans even if they don't make their own contribution.
- **Volunteer Hours:** Every employee receives 10 hours per year of paid time off to volunteer for charities of their choice.
- **Rewards and Recognitions:** Employees can earn contribution awards when managers or partners recognize them for excellence, outstanding effort and team work.

Entrepreneurship

As mentioned earlier in the chapter, the subject of entrepreneurship is only lightly discussed. There are many resources available for this sector as there are many variations of start-up businesses. For example, you might want to start a supply or transportation company or consulting firm as a disabled veteran or minority owned business. You may decide that you desire to become an owner/operator for your own truck.

Regardless, each city/county/state offers a variety of classes and seminars on how to successfully start these types of companies. The focus of this book is on transitioning into traditional logistics and logistics management jobs. If you should try entrepreneurship as a consultant or business, keep in mind the following concepts.

- You must be willing to take on risk to achieve success.
- There is no cook book and you cannot be a quitter.
- You need to have deep pockets or backing.
- Need to understand the business, tax and government laws, contracting associated with the business you are going pursuing.
- The measure of success for entrepreneurship is survivability 5 to 10 years out.
- Entrepreneurship is tough on the family and quality of life, unless there are other sources of income.
- You must be an optimist and pride yourself on doing things differently.

Market Place Comparison

Understanding how the commercial market place differs from the government is absolutely essential for your success in transitioning from the military. Knowing the value proposition is essential. Public organizations will perceive value through mission accomplishment with the least amount of hassle or disturbance. Private organizations will find value through seeking out the least cost and greatest capability, thereby enhancing the bottom line.

When looking at this question from the employee perspective, a term coined in England when comparing the public and private market place is "Sector

Envy". Universally, it appears that the "Grass is always greener" when looking at the opposing market place. With wildly varying risks, rewards, salaries, benefits and job security, "Sector Envy" is a very appropriate term among American workers as well. Let's compare the public and private market place as they relate to your personal desires.

With regard to "Sector Envy" it is interesting to note that there is an increase in the migration of workers moving back and forth between government agencies, DoD contractors and the commercial market place. Employees with contracting backgrounds make easy transitions into federal and civil servant jobs due to their skills, knowledge and abilities (SKAs). Generally, as a former service member becomes more familiar with commercial certifications and the new environment, they become more marketable in the commercial market place. Know that many have come before you and not only changed jobs, but also market places on multiple occasions.

So what do you need to know? You should be aware that there are many factors that separate public and private sectors. Fundamental environmental factors include: value proposition, business case, turnover challenges, and measures of success. Obvious factors are financial rewards, job security, benefits, and your ability to easily transition from the service. Some of the not so obvious factors are work-life balance, changing work environment, workload and career ladder. A few comparative environmental factors are given below:

Value proposition - Private sector managers worry about creating added value, while public-sector managers are often stifled by outdated, restrictive laws, regulations and policies that prevent rapid change or action.

Business case - In private industry there are clear well understood top to bottom goals and objectives. In the public sector goals are often divergent or disparate and can lead to confusion.

Turnover challenges - In government, leaders are often rotated in and out to ensure proper grooming and development of leadership. This thrash of leadership creates potential organizational change based on personality rather than achieving unity of movement towards goals and objectives. The corollary in the business world is a business merger or hostile takeover.

Key Performance Indicators (KPI) – In the absence of clearly understood business goals, government often invents measures of success that might be more aligned to short-term contractual and personal goals versus long-term business goals.

Stone walling – In the government setting, if a leader is not well received, senior civil servants will slow roll and wait out leadership change. This is especially true for political appointees or temporary military leadership. In the private sector there is no business case for this type of activity, as most companies will find this unacceptable.

These fundamental factors have huge environmental implications on workplace satisfaction. Figure 4.6 below compares positive responses from federal government employees against commercial-sector workers. These questions reflect the impact of some environmental factors previously discussed. The results show the public sector holds a slight edge over the commercial market place when employees are asked if they like the kind of work they do.[16] However, when it comes to recognition, training and supervisors, the commercial market place employees are a big winner.

QUESTION	GOVERNMENT-WIDE	COMMERCIAL MARKET PLACE	GAP
I like the kind of work I do.	81.2	75.0	6.2
My work gives me a feeling of personal accomplishment.	69.7	70.0	-0.3
I have enough information to do my job well.	69.3	71.0	-1.7
The people I work with cooperate to get the job done.	72.3	78.0	-5.7
I am given a real opportunity to improve my skills in my organization.	59.6	66.0	-6.4
Overall, how good a job do you feel is being done by your immediate supervisor/team leader?	65.8	73.0	-7.2
How satisfied are you with your opportunity to get a better job in your organization?	31.5	44.0	-12.5
How satisfied are you with the training you receive for your present job?	46.6	61.0	-14.4
How satisfied are you with the information you receive from management on what's going on in your organization?	44.8	60.0	-15.2
How satisfied are you with the recognition you receive for doing a good job?	42.6	64.0	-21.4

Figure 4.6 | Comparison - Federal to Commercial Work Satisfaction

Personal Market Place Satisfaction Scale

Having read the environmental factors, a side by side Market Place Satisfaction Scale is presented for your understanding of the remaining factor differences. When looking at the market places for future opportunities, it is beneficial to optimize where you search. Most of us do not have the latitude of time on our side to look for and, more importantly get a job. You can spend months searching through the job listings. We spend much of our lives at work, and it is worth being happy during that time. Additionally, about 20% of people leave their jobs every year, according to the Bureau of Labor Statistics.

If it is important for you not to be part of the statistic and continually rotate jobs, there are a few items to consider. A key consideration to staying in a particular job is your personal satisfaction. Sometimes we forget the "personal satisfaction" factor, as this will increase the chances of remaining in the same position. Make an honest evaluation and list the factors necessary for your workdays to be as enjoyable and rewarding as possible.

Nine satisfaction elements are utilized in the personal satisfaction scale. The definition of each element used in this tool is defined below in Figure 4.7.

ELEMENT	DEFINITION
Creative Environment	Opportunity/need to be creative in the job.
Financial Reward	Probability of salary increase and bonus based on success.
Change	Frequency of change expected on the job to maintain position.
Workload	Level of work expected to perform on the job to sustain position.
Career Ladder	Clearly defined job growth expectations and requirements.
Education Reimbursement	Financial reimbursement for additional education and certification.
Work/Life Balance	Based on rules and work week expectations, presents a level of work/life balance important to keep personnel satisfied.
Job Risk	Volatility and chance of losing your job due to issues outside of your control.
Benefits	Level of standardized benefits to include medical/dental, savings, retirement, vacation time, education, etc.
Ease of Transition	Determination of transitional ease for former service members.

Figure 4.7 | Factor Definitions

To assist in your organization of these personal satisfaction elements, the following market place satisfaction scale is presented. Columns represent the four market places covered in this chapter: Civil Service, DoD Contractor, Commercial, and Entrepreneur. Rows represent typical elements as they relate to the market place. The scale is presented below in Figure 4-8. Probabilities are plotted for each factor in each marketplace based upon whether the element has a high-medium-low likelihood of influence in the marketplace. Data for the grid is based upon years of discussion and experience. There will always be exceptions, but for your purposes, the table should prove helpful to those in transition from the military, offering a foundation that can be customized based upon your own experiences.

At a glance, two items that might be of importance to you are security and work/life balance. If these two are important to you, you may gravitate towards the civil service work. If you enjoy risk and desire a highly competitive and potentially creative environment, you may align yourself with commercial industry, or perhaps, even entrepreneurship.

When considering all the elements of the table, you will notice that the civil service marketplace offers more stability and you can have relative confidence that you will be able to remain in the position, with a standard offering of benefits, salary and a pro-active work/life balance. If you desire to climb the corporate ladder and create an opportunity of accelerated promotions and desire to try to capture a better than average salary due to your creative mindset, you will be better served in either the Commercial of Entrepreneurial markets.

Finally, the scale roughly correlates with personality types. You may have previously identified with either 'Type A' or 'Type B' behaviors. 'Type A' personalities are typically ambitious, rigidly organized, high achieving, "workaholics", multi-taskers, highly motivated, insist on deadlines, and hate both delays and ambivalence.

Contrastingly, 'Type B' personalities live at a lower stress level and typically work steadily, enjoying achievement but do not become stressed if immediate gratification is not present. They may be creative and enjoy exploring ideas and concepts and are often reflective.

Use Figure 4.8 to assist you in developing thoughts on which market place may provide the best landing space for you after the service based on your personality and style. Take a few moments and ponder the difference to ensure you are pursuing the best match for your lifestyle.

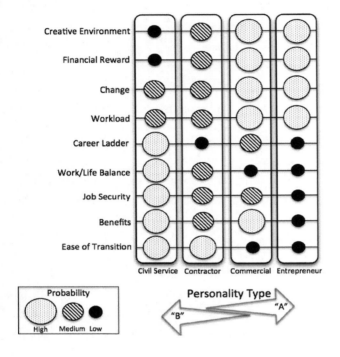

Figure 4.8 | Personal Market Place Satisfaction

Assessment #5 *(Market Place)*

Figure 4.9 is the fifth and final assessment in the book, exploring personal factors that influence which market place offers the best alignment to your interests. You may answer the assessment questions here. When you are ready to analyze them, refer to Chapter 5. You can also utilize the companion guide to this book, available for download and print out on-line at Gr8MilitaryLog.com. Read each question and choose the correct answer for your current situation.

5: MARKET PLACE	Strongly Disagree	Disagree	Neither Agree OR Disagree	Agree	Strongly Agree
Potential salary increase is more important to me than job security.					
A potentially stressful work place and long hours are not concerns for me.					
Creativity and innovation are more important than procedures.					
I am excited by the prospect of leaving public service and trying something different in the private sector.					
I desire promotions based on personal performance rather than on pay scales and longevity.					
Switching companies or changing positions frequently are not concerns for me.					
Feeling safe from competition and losing my job are factors I rarely think about.					
I desire to work in an environment that rewards my innovative behavior and 'out of the box' thinking.					
An environment where I can share and use my military experiences and knowledge is not overly important to me.					
I prefer driving or "making" my career path rather than waiting on promotion.					

Figure 4.9 | Market Place Assessment

Summary

Once comfortable with the basics, knowledge of the market place will help you gain a competitive advantage and keep you from proceeding down the wrong path for your next career. A few departing thoughts are presented as you progress in your job search and transition:

1. If you have a target market place in mind, make sure your resume is tailored to the markets you desire and that your network and connections will be able to assist.

2. You can inquire and ask questions at the end of an interview such as how the company views different positions; how risk adverse the company is; how mature their documentation processes are; what tools are used; what career path options are open to someone starting in your position and what criteria is used to measure and advance.

3. Once at the job, think out-of-the-box. Do not just go into the job and expect a list of daily activities to perform. In the military, you had to adapt. Now is the time to utilize that trait.

4. Gain confidence in the new position by understanding both the official and unofficial political fabric of your environment.

5. Understand your peers and your boss(es). As you master your expected job skills, continue to branch out as far as possible to other divisions, groups, and teams. This knowledge will increase your overall understanding and appreciation of the organization, as a holistic view will assist you in evaluating the position you are in and how it connects with your expectations and goals.

The choice to prepare yourself and perform good market place selection is yours to make. You are encouraged to continue to grow your understanding of these different sectors. In the story below, discover how one woman, after being an Army Supply officer, a contractor and working in public service found her military experience as a water purification platoon leader absolutely invaluable later in life as the Mayor of Saint Pete Beach.

You too will find your experiences invaluable as you make your transition.

MAJ Maria Lowe, USA, Ret
Success Through Water

LIVING ON AN ISLAND, IT IS NOT SURPRISING THAT THE LIFE OF MAJ MARIA LOWE, RET, THE MAYOR OF SAINT PETE BEACH HAS A STRONG CONNECTION WITH WATER. As Maria Vedder grew up in Monticello, Georgia, many of her favorite pastimes revolved around water and water sport. Graduating from the United States Military Academy at West Point on the Hudson, Maria entered into the Army as Quartermaster Officer. After attending the Army Logistics School at Fort Lee, Virginia, Maria led a Reverse Osmosis Water Purification Unit (ROWPU) Platoon in Korea, with a mission of producing water for over 15,000 soldiers on the peninsula during wartime. Later, she would serve as a Commander of a Supply and Services Company in the United States and Egypt. One of Maria's many great accomplishments was serving on a Female Engagement Team, in Afghanistan. Talking with Afghani women about their personal security issues as they related to their families, Maria found water to be one of their most important and compelling concerns. Beyond working to assist in this area, Maria worked with the engagement team to assist in providing medical treatment and enhancing some education methods.

During her campaign for mayor, she stated "My skills are transferable", making it clear that she is "100% St. Pete Beach". These comments obviously resonated with the populace, as she was elected in March of 2014. Little did she know how uniquely qualified she really was, quickly learning one of the greatest issues facing the Saint Pete Beach is the movement of fresh water to the residents and sewer removal from the islands. Maria enthusiastically states her ROWPU platoon leader experience gives her the ability to understand the complexities discussed at council meetings by the hydraulic and civil engineers. Maria is grateful for her initial quartermaster and Army experiences.

She believes a leader needs to listen closely, be fully-informed, and represent everyone with respect. MAJ Maria Lowe, Ret, has committed her entire adult life in service to our country. Duty, honor and country are not just words to Maria, they are her core values."

The Right Fit

NOW IT IS YOUR TURN. While reading this book you have gained focus of your strengths, simultaneously learning about the job market and the commercial logistics profession. You have the logic behind positioning yourself for the job market and you have gained the confidence to attack the competition. Now you will organize these elements together to shift your mental posture from the defensive to the offensive.

Combining the knowledge gained from this book with the personal information you collected through the assessments will facilitate the creation of a high impact personal strategic roadmap. This exciting instrument provides directed self-awareness while gaining an understanding of your strengths and the confidence required to take on the next challenge.

Several tools are introduced in this chapter. The first tool is for charting your assessment scores collected in earlier chapters. This tool identifies those

> *"One defends when his strength is inadequate, he attacks when it is abundant."*
>
> **Sun Tzu 孫子**
> *The Art of War*

personal areas that can be exploited (strengths) and those areas for possible improvement. The second tool is the Personal Strategic Roadmap. Assessment scores that reflect areas for possible improvement will be transferred onto your personal strategic roadmap. This roadmap will be used continuously as you track, monitor, and achieve your personal goals.

To gain the best results, work through the process with honest introspection and reflection. Completing these steps enable your preference for market place, career and level of readiness for transitioning into commercial logistics. There are three steps involved:

1. Gaining an understanding and control of personal information and capabilities that you have, thereby reducing risks of the unknown.

2. Analyzing outcomes of each assessment to identify what you already possess in your "kit bag" for successful resume writing, interviewing, and transition.

3. Setting goals based on those areas you choose for improvement. These improvements are to be charted, monitored, and tracked on the Personal Strategic Roadmap until they are achieved.

Step One - Gaining Control of Your Personal Information (The UNK-UNK Chart)

In certain areas of the military and civilian world, the UNK-UNK chart is used to depict information available about organizations. The title of the UNK-UNK chart is derived from using "UNK" as an abbreviation to "Unknown". The chart is useful not only to military planning and operation groups, but to commercial organizations performing risk analysis. When you transform an organizational construct to a personal perspective, the UNK-UNK chart is useful in identifying and understanding what you know and don't know about yourself.

The UNK-UNK chart is broken into four quadrants (Figure 5.1). Quadrants are defined with regard to the terms "Known" and "Unknown". These terms refer to a general understanding of information an organization has awareness of ("knowns") and information not known ("unknowns"). When you array these two terms on both sides of the chart and step through the following analysis, an approach to reducing your "unknowns" begins to unfold. Organizations categorize information as follows: What information they know (KK); what they know that they don't know (KU); what they do not know that they know (UK); and what information they do not know exists and are completely unaware of (UU).

The upper left quadrant (KK-information you know you know) is a very valuable commodity. In this quadrant, the organization is "self-aware" and this knowledge can be exploited. By way of a military example, if you know you know the location of the enemy, you plan and move to contact to destroy the enemy at this location. Similarly, in business, a corporation would want to try to exploit its capabilities in the marketplace if they knew they had a competitive advantage. From a personal perspective, your skills, characteristics, abilities, and sense for the type of marketplace you want to pursue are very valuable. Acknowledge and exploit this information on your resume and during your interviews to achieve the best career alignment.

The upper right quadrant (KU, or, know what you do not know) denotes an organization, which understands they do not have certain information elements needed for success. Capturing these information elements provides tremendous value for study, assessment and improvement within the organization. For example, if a company does not have market information they consider valuable, they work to resolve the information shortfall in an effort to gain a competitive advantage. From a personal perspective, knowing that you do not have

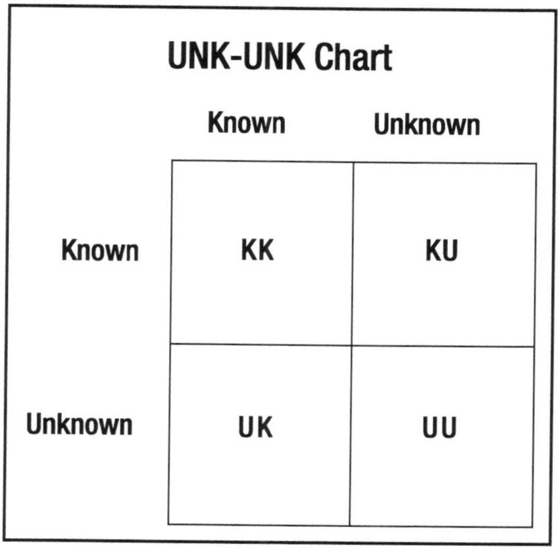

Figure 5.1 | UNK-UNK Chart

a capability is of vital importance. During an interview, not knowing the hiring manager's expectations and how the organization perceives value can bring the interview process to a halt. Take some time to know the customer to try and reduce the risk associated with this quadrant. KU elements become goals for your Personal Strategic Roadmap. Achieving these associated goals turn KUs into KKs, increasing your competitive edge.

The bottom left quadrants (UK, or, you don't know what you know), is very harmful in combat. To avoid this outcome, military organizations employ a term or slogan "Who else needs to know?" When critical information is not shared, it can cause mission failure. A company may know they have a capability, but fail to see its value or how to exploit the capability, and their competitor gets to market faster. Applying this quadrant to your personal transition, you want to ensure you have uncovered your capabilities, even the ones that you do not expect to be of significant marketability. During interviews, take time to exploit and share your accomplishments, certifications, and experiences as they relate to the company.

Finally, the bottom right quadrant (UU, or information you don't know that you don't know) is all about reaction. "Ignorance is bliss" is a common cliché associated with this quadrant. In this quadrant, action occurs and change happens rapidly if you do not have the information necessary for counter-action. It is the riskiest of quadrants as there are unexpected outcomes, because

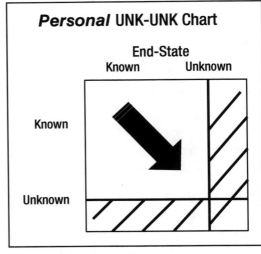

Figure 5.2 | Competitive Gain

you could not anticipate events. In the corporate world, while you continue the status quo, your competitor may develop something viable and exploit the market opportunity before you ever realize what happened!

Why go through the exercise of analyzing the UNK-UNK chart? Your objective is to reduce the size of any unknowns and associated risks. As shown in Figure 5.2, reducing the level of "unexpected unknowns" and turning them into "knowns" is the best method to increase your personal edge and confidence. There will always be "unknown" shortcomings, but it is essential to reduce the 'unknown' quadrant as much as possible by expanding other quadrants, making your 'known' area as large as possible. For this to happen, reflect upon your undiscovered skills and characteristics.

With the knowledge of the UNK-UNK chart, let us use the remaining tools of this book to help you determine what areas you need to exploit and what you need to improve upon.

Step Two - Understanding Assessment Results

Analyzing assessment outcomes assists in determining what you already have in your "kit bag" for transitional success. In each prior chapter, assessments were provided in five key transitional areas, summarized in Figure 5.3 below. As mentioned in the introduction, your assessment results should have been documented in the gem formats, available through the free downloadable companion guide found at GR8MilitaryLog.com.

Assessment Type	Chapter	Topic Areas
Personal Characteristics	2	Leadership, motivation, creativity, managing others, personal growth, organizational skills, repeatability, working with others, visionary
Environmental	2	Family, re-locations, financial obligations, retirement objectives, schools, faith, etc.
Timing	2	Service goals met, training/certification goals, time remaining, commitment, financial preparedness
Skills	3	Military skills, educations, certifications, credentials, jobs
Market Place	4	Civil Service, contractor (DoD), commercial market place, analysis based on income, stress competition predictability, longevity, mental growth, benefits

Figure 5.3 | Assessment Topics

Star Charting

To assess your strengths and improvement areas, a chart in the form of a star will be created utilizing the companion guide. Begin building the star by charting each assessment score on a 'gem' (Figure 5.4) on the y-axis. The y-axis represents your readiness to transition, or how 'ready' you are to transition from the military. For each assessment, use the question number and plot answer results on the gem axis. It is highly recommended that you use the free companion guide for the assessment. However, the five gems and the star can be manually recreated.

When plotting the results of your assessments, you will likely find more than one answer on an axis point. Simply cluster the plotted points. Analysis of each assessment gem offers a journey to unfolding your personal roadmap. In turn, the roadmap will guide you to the best-suited career path in the best-suited market place.

Companion Guide at:
GR8MilitaryLog.com

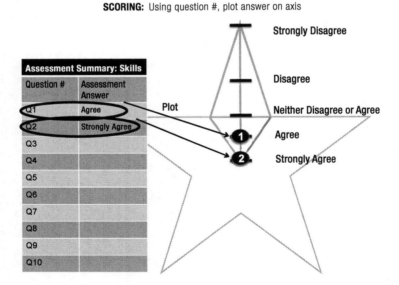

Figure 5.4 | Star Chart Mapping

Once each gem is completed, combine all gems with the associated assessment results to build the Star Chart provided in the companion guide to view your aggregate results (Figure 5.5). When combined, these plotted assessment results form the shape of a star, resulting in a personal index. Your personal index summarizes key indicators from your personal, environmental, timing, marketplace and skills assessments; clearly stating your readiness, marketplace, and ease of transition from the military. With this knowledge you will understand the best options to pursue, given your strategy goals and objectives.

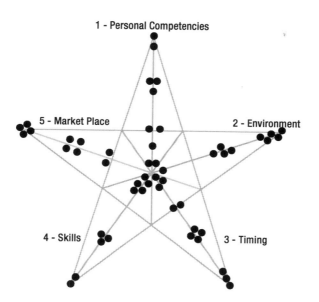

Figure 5.5 | Star Chart Assessment Results

Within the star is the shape of a pentagon (Figure 5.6). Assessment answers plotted within the pentagon represent your strengths. These strengths are items to be exploited in your job search and interviews. Assessment answers plotted outside of the pentagon suggest that these are potential areas important to improve, and to be transferred to your Personal Strategic Roadmap discussed in step Three. Once the analysis of your assessment answers has been completed, you are ready to move on to creating your personal strategic roadmap.

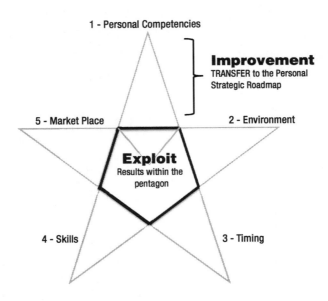

Figure 5.6 | Star Chart Areas for Improvement and Exploitation

Step Three - Setting your Goals

Next, use the Personal Strategic Roadmap to capture your noted areas of improvement from the assessments and increase your probability of transition success. The outcome of this step will be the Personal Strategic Roadmap shown in Appendix E. A full size, editable Personal Strategic Roadmap is also available in the free online companion guide. There are four main sections to the roadmap as shown in Figure 5.7.

Personal Strategic Roadmap Sections	
1.	Improvements
2.	Vision
3.	Goals and Success
4.	Commit and Attest

Figure 5.7 | Strategic Roadmap Improvements

Use the Personal Strategic Roadmap to list your goals and establish how you will achieve these goals, along with setting the target timeframes for each goal. It is on your roadmap that you will track and monitor these goals until achieved. You will need to monitor your goals on a recurring basis and track your progress. As goals are met, reward yourself, remove each of them from the roadmap and transfer each of these goals to your resume or exploit during your next interview.

Follow the next repeatable actions to complete each critical section of the roadmap and gain the full benefit.

a. Section 1 - Capture Improvements:

As mentioned in Step 2, identify all assessment answers outside of the pentagon. Transfer these improvements to the top portion of the roadmap in the improvements section. It is important to capture all improvements from all assessments. For example, plotted results from the Skills Assessment Gem determine a need to achieve a commercial logistics certification. In the improvements section of the Personal Strategic Road Map, list those items in Line 4, skills as shown in Figure 5.8 below:

Personal Strategic Road Map v1.0	
Vision: Obtain A Project Management career th	
Mission: Develop a course of action to create a satisfyin	
ASSESSMENT RESULTS ➡	Areas for Change/Improvement
	Change / Improvement # 1
1. Environmental/Spousal	
2. Characteristics	
3. Timing	
4. Skills	Need to get my APICS ® Certified Supply Chain Professional (CSCP)
5. Market Place ☐ Commercial ☐ Contract ☐ Civil Service	

(Left vertical label: **IMPROVEMENTS**)

Figure 5.8 | Strategic Map Improvements

b. Section 2 - State Your Personal Vision:

Based upon your reading and the improvements captured from Section 1, reflect upon how you desire to work on these improvements. Some of the improvements might be independent of others, such as your interest to take a class to achieve a certification. Some improvements might be best combined with others. For example, you may desire to focus your job search in the Civil Service market place and geographically target your job search to the northeast region of the United States where you can be close to a major airport. To adequately capture the influences in achieving your personal vision, write what you want to achieve with the qualifiers that are important to you in the vision section. Include some or all of the following: Job place/location (CONUS/OCONUS, state, city), timeframe, marketplace focus, salary range, possible positions, risk level you are willing to take, industries, and any other considerations. An example is given in Figure 5.9 below:

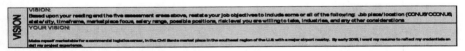

Figure 5.9 | Strategic Map Vision

c. Section 3 - Create Goals and Identify Success:

Now you will create goals from your areas of improvement. If there are more than four improvements, it is recommended that you focus on three or four most important to you. Further, take into consideration the level of effort and time associated with the success of achieving the goal. Some improvement/goals might be independent of one another, such as your interest to take a class to achieve a certification. Some improvement/goals might be best grouped with one or more improvements to clarify and better define success. Transform your improvements into goals that can be achieved with an identified timeframe and measured. For example, transform the improvement 'get a logistics certification' to the goal of 'APICS ® Certified Supply Chain Professional (CSCP)'. Post the steps you need to take to achieve the goal, as well as a specific timeframe that you want to achieve the goal as shown in Figure 5.10 below.

GOALS: Pick most important improvement areas from above you want to focus on, depending on level of complexity, learning, or duration (i.e., school). * List: goals, align which Assessment it ties, year/quarter/month expected to achieve, and present your achievement path (how you will get to your goal and possible								
PRIORITY	GOAL STATEMENT	ASSESSMENT TIE	PATH TO ACHIEVING GOAL	YEAR/QTR/MO TO ACHIEVE (personally set)				ACHIEVED ?
GOAL # 1	APICS ® Certified Supply Chain Professional (CSCP)	__ Environment __ Characteristics __ Timing __ Skills __ Market Place	I will research classes available free of charge from military and other organizations, study, apply for certificatio, take the exam and pass!!	Q3- 2015 Class	Q4 - 2015 Application	Q1 - 2016 Take Exam	Update Resume with New Cert	YES / NO Reschedule or no longer need Date ____
GOAL # 2		__ Environment __ Characteristics __ Timing __ Skills __ Market Place						YES / NO Reschedule or no longer need Date ____
GOAL # 3		__ Environment __ Characteristics __ Timing __ Skills __ Market Place						YES / NO Reschedule or no longer need Date ____
GOAL # 4		__ Environment __ Characteristics __ Timing __ Skills __ Market Place						YES / NO Reschedule or no longer need Date ____

Figure 5.10 | Strategic Map Goals and Achievement

Set a reminder through your calendar to review your progress on each goal listed. Depending on the urgency of the goal, review your roadmap weekly. Do this religiously and do not falter. Look at your roadmap and ask yourself – "What progress or steps have I taken to move towards achieving this goal?" Once progress is achieved, make notes in the "Path to Achieving Goal." If there are outside circumstances that have caused a slip to the right of your scheduled achievement – annotate and move on. Ask yourself, "Was it a slip based upon not working to achieve the goal, or an outside circumstance that was out of your control?" Assess the situation and adjust your goal schedule accordingly in the "Year/Quarter/Month to Achieve" area. If you achieve the goal, mark 'yes' and celebrate! You are that much closer to an easier and successful transition.

d. Section 4 - Commit and Attest:

Once you identify what you want to do, annotate it, then sign and date the roadmap as shown in Figure 5.11 below. If you have a family member or a mentor you want to watch and monitor with you, get them to co-sign. Why? You need to remind yourself and your family that you are committed to achieving these goals and that you want to remain accountable. Make a copy of this form and hang it on your refrigerator or keep it in your wallet. Set a repeatable time for a thorough review of your personal strategic roadmap, preferably with the cosigner and revisit the courses of actions if necessary.

While this is a roadmap that captures the steps you need to transition from the military, the goals themselves are not cast in stone. If for some reason a goal becomes overcome by events, do not see this as a failure. Carefully assess the situation and the circumstances surrounding the reason why the goal is not achievable and take it off the list. Revisit Sections A through D and transform other improvement areas as they develop into goals. Through achieving these goals, you will increase your 'knowns', thereby increasing your opportunity for job transition and success.

Figure 5.11 | Strategic Map Sign and Attest

In this chapter, you gain an understanding of your strengths and weaknesses as identified in the assessments provided earlier in the book. These weaknesses are marked for improvement and are translated into goals and annotated in the Personal Strategic Roadmap. Your strengths become areas to highlight on a resume and in an interview.

The bottom line is to increase your "knowns" and reduce the risk of the "unknowns" through preparation, planning and analysis. The more assessment results within the pentagon, the higher probability that you are ready to transition with minimum issues and stress. Use your strategic roadmap to achieve areas of improvement. This actionable exercise will increase the probability of success as you look and interview for jobs in the right logistics market place that best fits you!

Many external resources, models, examples and anecdotes are provided for your consideration throughout this book. It is up to you to select and use the tools that best fit your situation. Transitioning from the military is never easy, but if you can find some nuggets within this book that you can use, then the book will have fulfilled its purpose. Finally, just know you are not alone. Many have come before you and have made the transition. Draw upon others to assist you with their transitional stories through GR8MilitaryLog.com. Just like the case study below, you can and will be successful in the next exciting phase of your life – plan on it!

McPO John McGriff, USN, Ret
Successful Transition Secrets

A SAILOR ONCE STATED, "I HAVE SPREAD THE MANTLE OF MY NATION OVER THE OCEAN, AND WILL GUARD HER FOREVER. I am her heritage, and yours. I am the American Sailor." McPO John McGriff, Ret, grew up in a family of US Navy dating back to the second World War, who believed this quote to be manifest through their service.

Initially, serving in warehouses and basic inventory management, John progressed in rank, working in the more complex areas of financial management, production planning and forecasting. Later in his career, he began to manage shipping and receiving of large scale inventory facilities, while learning many aspects of contracting. John served out the remainder of his career as a senior level logistics manager, running large scale warehouses and shipboard operations with all associated material handling equipment management, operations and safety functions. Believing he had fulfilled his purpose, John reluctantly left his family's tradition of Naval service after 30 years.

As John transitioned from uniform, he considered multiple career fields to include law enforcement. Having acceptance and scheduled for boot camp with the Florida Highway Patrol, John was offered a position from Honeywell as a supply officer with the Navy Supply Support for Maritime Prepositioned Ships Program at Blount Island near Jacksonville. While he initially had a strong desire to enter public service as a state trooper, he soon learned that becoming a DoD contractor with a commercial company had greater pay and potentially benefits. With the Navy retirement benefits, John decided to work for a Fortune 100 Company in the commercial sector, having determined that pay outweighed the professed state trooper stability and work environment.

John's desire to share his many years' of experiences with others is invaluable. He knows that there are companies that are very willing to hire military logisticians and the transitioning service member just needs search to find the right fit. Some companies like seasoned professionals. Other companies prefer younger logistical workers, to gain a long term investment. Companies will gladly hire veterans for actual worker and supervisory positions. However, John's experience has taught him that some companies will want the greatest return on investment (ROI) after 12-18 months of initial training for new positions.

John's thoughts on education are simple. You need a degree. However, knowing how it relates to the career field is essential. He confidently states a company's ROI for hiring a 25 year old Bachelor of Science graduate is much higher than a 46 year old MBA graduate. In John's experience, many companies have very few corporate managers that did not come up from inside. Therefore, he believes very few senior officer or senior enlisted are hired directly into a corporate position. Therefore, the hybrid field of DoD contracting may prove more lucrative for many senior transitioning service members.

John believes some of the best things you can do to make your yourself marketable are to gain a vast experience in many elements of logistics management, have a great work ethic, be accountable, be customer focused, and display maturity and leadership in all aspects of your life. He wishes all service members tremendous success with their transition endeavors into the lucrative career field of logistics.

Appendix

Appendix A – Lexicon

This lexicon provides a few military terms and definitions with associated commercial logistics management terminology. The commercial logistics definitions are derived from multiple sources, to include Wikipedia and supplychain247.com.

COMMERCIAL/MILITARY LOGISTICS LEXICON		
KEY COMMERCIAL TERM	**COMMERCIAL DEFINITION**	**MILITARY EQUIVALENT**
3PL	A third-party, or contract, logistics company. A firm to which logistics services are outsourced.	Contract Organization; i.e., KBR, Dyncorp
Agreement	A contract with a customer that serves as the basis for work authorization.	Customer Order / Reimbursable Order
Break-bulk Cargo	Cargo in-between bulk and containerized, that must be handled piece-by-piece by terminal workers (stevedores).	Any commodity that, because of its weight, dimensions, or non-compatibility with other cargo, must be shipped by mode other than MILVAN or SEAVAN. - Joint Pub1-02

KEY COMMERCIAL TERM	COMMERCIAL DEFINITION	MILITARY EQUIVALENT
FOB (Free-on-Board) Point	Point at which ownership of freight changes hands from shipper to consignee.	A term of sale defining who is to incur transportation charges for the shipment, who is to control the shipment movement, or where title to the goods passes to the buyer; originally meant "free on board ship."
Freight Bill-of-Lading (Freight Bill, BL or BoL)	A document providing a binding contract between a shipper and a carrier for the transportation of freight.	The acknowledgment of the receipt of goods for movement by the carrier and the contract for the movement. (AR 310-25)
Freight Forwarder	An agency that receives freight from a shipper and then arranges for transportation with one or more carriers for transport to the consignee.	An individual, firm, partnership, corporation, company or association other than a railroad, motor or water carrier, which represents itself as a common carrier
Hi-lo	Container yard jargon for a forklift truck used for heavy lifting of containers.	Rough Terrain Container Handler (RTCH)
Loss and Damage	Loss or damage of freight shipments while in transit or in a carrier-operated warehouse.	Discrepancy
Private Carrier	Owned and operated by a shipper. Usually refers to private trucking fleets.	Contract Carrier
Purchase Order	A transaction representing a legally binding purchase.	Obligations
Requisition	A transaction representing an intent to purchase goods and services as indicated by the completion and approval of a requisition.	Commitment

KEY COMMERCIAL TERM	COMMERCIAL DEFINITION	MILITARY EQUIVALENT
Transportation Broker	An agency that obtains negotiated large-volume transportation rates from carriers, and resells this capacity to shippers. Unlike freight forwarders, will not handle freight and owns no pickup/delivery equipment or storage facilities.	Military Surface Deployment and Distribution Command (SDDC) provides ocean terminal, commercial ocean liner service and traffic management services to deploy, sustain and redeploy U.S. forces on a global basis.

Appendix B – Logistic Certification Organizations

The following table provides a listing of logistic certifying organizations and their associated websites. These organizations typically require registration. Once you have become a member of the organization, you can then go through there certification process. Often testing is performed at local testing centers like Prometric or Pearson VUE.

The certification process typically consists of the following steps:

1. Perform some personal analysis and determine your desired certification.
2. Join and/or register with the organization that provides your desired certification.
3. Study their process for certification.
4. Find materials and study for certification exam.
5. Request an Authority to Test.
6. Schedule the exam.
7. Take the exam and celebrate your success!

Remember, you may qualify for VA Test reimbursement.

Certifying Organization	Website
American Society for Quality (ASQ)	www.asq.org
American Society of Transportation and Logistics, Inc. (AST&L)	www.astl.org
APICS The Association for Operations Management	www.apics.org
Automotive Service Excellence (ASE)	www.ase.com
Computing Technology Industry Association (CompTIA)	www.comptia.org
In-Plant Printing and Mailing Association	www.ipma.org
Institute for Supply Management (ISM)	www.comptia.org
Institute of Certified Professional Managers (ICPM)	www.instituteforsupplymanagement.org
Institute of Hazardous Materials Management (IHMM)	www.ihmm.org
Institute of Packaging Professionals (IoPP)	www.iopp.org
Mail Systems Management Association	www.msmanational.org
Manufacturing Skill Standards Council (MSSC)	www.msscusa.org
Professional Evaluation and Certification Board (PECB)	www.pecb.org
Society for Maintenance and Reliability Professionals (SMRP)	www.smrp.org
The International Society of Logistics (SOLE)	www.sole.org
Universal Public Procurement Certification Council (UPPCC)	www.uppcc.org

Appendix C – Alternative Logistical Career Fields

This appendix defines other logistic career fields that may be of interest to you during your transition.

Position	Location
Procurement logistics	Consists of activities such as market research, requirements planning, make-or-buy decisions, supplier management, ordering, and order controlling.
Distribution logistics	Delivery of the finished products to the customer. It consists of order processing, warehousing, and transportation.
Disposal logistics	Reduce logistics cost and enhance service related to the disposal of waste produced during the operation of a business.
Reverse logistics	Operations related to the reuse of products and materials. The reverse logistics process includes the management and the sale of surpluses, as well as products being returned to vendors from buyers.
Green Logistics	Attempts to measure and minimize the ecological impact of logistics activities.
RAM Logistics	Concerned with highly complex technical systems for which Reliability, Availability and Maintainability are essential, ex: weapon systems and supercomputers.
Asset Control Logistics	Companies in the retail channels, both organized retailers and suppliers, often deploy assets required for the display, preservation, promotion of their products.
Emergency logistics	Logistics management of specific time-critical modes of transport used to move goods or objects rapidly in the event of an emergency.
Production Logistics	Production logistics aims to ensure that each machine and workstation receives the right product in the right quantity and quality at the right time, often in a factory setting.

Appendix D – Salary Considerations

Congratulations, you made it to the salary stage of the interview! Salary negotiations are tricky and sensitive. Don't sweat, but be prepared. Research a fair salary. Understand the benchmarks for your position. Arm yourself with salary information. Spend adequate time conducting research to find out average salary ranges for similar jobs in the area, industry, and geography. Then decide on an appropriate salary range. To determine a realistic salary range, forego any thoughts about how many kids you have in college, your boat payment, or your upcoming European vacation. Instead, research and calculate an appropriate salary. It is also good practice to identify your "can't live with" point. Think about the reasons why you would not be willing to accept a lower amount. Many websites offer ideas on how to establish these salary points. If at a loss, a few ideas are presented below which offer some insights to consider.

Determine the average salary for your position at your desired location. Figure D-1 below is a sample developed from 2014 United States salary statistics from Salary.com. Study the table and cross check other sources to provide you salary expectations. Remember, title, experience and certification are all variables and the table below is given as a guide.

Position	Location	10%	25%	50%	75%	90%
Warehouse Supervisor	Tampa, FL	$39,630	$46,247	$53,514	$61,051	$67,913
Warehouse Supervisor	San Francisco, CA	$50,763	$59,238	$68,547	$78,201	$86,991
Warehouse Supervisor	El Paso, TX	$34,983	$40,823	$47,238	$53,891	$59,948
Warehouse Manager	Tampa, FL	$52,705	$61,832	$71,857	$85,251	$97,445
Warehouse Manager	San Francisco, CA	$67,511	$79,202	$92,043	$109,199	$124,820
Warehouse Manager	El Paso, TX	$46,524	$54,581	$63,430	$75,253	$86,017

Figure D1 | Sample Salary Averages for 2015 (Salary.com)

Certifications and Experience may improve your salary threshold. Often, employers will pay more for certification. Sometimes, certification is the only way to get your foot in the door. The goodness of certifications is that it differentiates you in the marketplace and gives you a competitive advantage in the job market; or may get you into the interview.

Remember, many logistical workers experience salary increases because of their certification and because of their prior military experience. There is no guaranteeing a higher salary for certification and experience, but you can certainly use these as a basis for negotiation.

Appendix E – Personal Strategic Road Map

Personal Strategic Road Map v1.0

GotMilitaryPM ®

Vision: Obtain A Project Management career that meets or exceeds my expectations

Mission: Develop a course of action to create a satisfying and financially lucrative transitional outcome.

Transition Date: _____
RoadMap Initiation Date: _____

IMPROVEMENTS

ASSESSMENT RESULTS ➡ Areas for Change/Improvement from Star Chart results outside the pentagon

	Change / Improvement #1	Change / Improvement #2	Change / Improvement #3	Change / Improvement #4
1. Environmental/Spousal				
2. Characteristics				
3. Timing				
4. Skills				
5. Market Place				

□ Commercial
□ Contract
□ Civil Service

VISION

Based upon your reading and the five assessment areas above, restate your job objectives to include some or all of the following: Job place/location (CONUS/OCONUS, state/city, timeframe, marketplace focus, salary range, possible positions, risk level you are willing to take, industries, and any other considerations

YOUR VISION:

GOALS & ACHIEVEMENT

GOALS:
Pick most important improvement areas from above you want to focus on, depending on level of complexity, learning, or duration [i.e., school).
* List: goals, align which Assessment it ties, year/quarter/month expected to achieve, and present your achievement path (how you will get to your goal and possible steps if necessary

PRIORITY	GOAL STATEMENT	ASSESSMENT TIE	PATH TO ACHIEVING GOAL	YEAR/QTR/MO TO ACHIEVE (personally set)	ACHIEVED ?
GOAL # 1	enter goal here.....	Environment / Characteristics / Timing / Skills / Market Place	enter steps.....		YES / NO — Reschedule or no longer need? Date ____
GOAL # 2		Environment / Characteristics / Timing / Skills / Market Place			YES / NO — Reschedule or no longer need? Date ____
GOAL # 3		Environment / Characteristics / Timing / Skills / Market Place			YES / NO — Reschedule or no longer need? Date ____
GOAL # 4		Environment / Characteristics / Timing / Skills / Market Place			YES / NO — Reschedule or no longer need? Date ____

ATTEST

Date of Next Review: _____

Signature: _____ Date: _____
Spouse Signature: _____ Date: _____

GotMilitaryPM.com
©Copyright 2014

Acknowledgments

Sitting at a fest table in Giessen Germany 25 years ago, who would have known that 1LT Dave Buchanan would collaborate on this book. Dave Buchanan's subject matter expertise and assistance have been absolutely instrumental and we cannot thank him enough.

To the many others that provided support, editing and knowledge, Sandy and I owe a debt of gratitude. We extend a very special thanks to Bob Kennedy, Cam Miles, Dennis Barletta, Keith Jones, LCDR Jeretta Dillon, LTC Keith Poynor, Bob Radiz, McPO (R) John McGriff, Larry Bamberger, Hal, Pat and Kellie Hicks. Each of you provided very special texture and granularity to this work, while giving us your valuable time and experience. We are eternally grateful. This has not been an easy undertaking. Knowing that you believe in supporting transitioning service members and our approach to providing assistance and knowledge, made this a much easier task.

Jay Hicks and Sandy Cobb

End Notes

Chapter 1

1 . "10 Reasons to Consider a Career in Logistics", Evans Distribution, 2014, https://www.evansdist .com/Top10_LogisticsCareers.aspx (accessed June 25, 2015).

2 . "Occupational Outlook Handbook: Logistics," Bureau of Labor Statistics, Department of Labor, January 8, 2014, http://www.bls.gov/ooh/business-and-financial/logisticians.htm#tab-1 (accessed February 25, 2015).

Chapter 2

1. Christopher, Shane, "GI Jobs – Why are employers Seeking Military Experience", G.I.Jobs, April 28, 2014, http://www.gijobs.com/employers-seeking-military-experience (accessed July 10, 2014).

2. "Top 100 Military Friendly Employers", Show Your Stripes, 2013, http://www.showyourstripes. org/resources/top100military.html, (accessed June 25, 2015).

3. Society of Human Resource Managers, "Employing Military Personnel and Recruiting Veterans, What HR can do," SHRM, June 23, 2010, http://www.shrm.org/research/surveyfindings/ documents/10-0531%20military%20program%20report_fnl.pdf (accessed June 25, 2015).

4. Biro, Meghan, "5 Reasons Leaders Hire Veterans", November, 2012, http://www.forbes.com/ sites/meghanbiro/2012/11/04/5-reasons-leaders-hire-veterans, (accessed June 25, 2015).

5. Lerner, Michele, "How big should your emergency fund be?," Bankrate.com, Mar 6, 2012, http://www.bankrate.com/finance/savings/how-big-should-emergency-fund-be.aspx (accessed February 18, 2015).

6 . Doyle, Alison, "Resume Types: Chronological, Functional, Combination", About.com, 2015, http://jobsearch.about.com/od/resumes/p/resumetypes.htm, (accessed June 25, 2015).

7. "Professional Organizations and Associations and Supply Chain/Logistics Industry Associations", University of Maryland, 2015, http://www.rhsmith.umd.edu/faculty-research/academic-departments/logistics-business-public-policy/research/professional, (accessed June 25, 2015).

8 . "About Us", International Association of Public Health Logisticians, 2015, http://iaphl.org, (accessed June 25, 2015).

Chapter 3

1. Tepic, J., Tanackov, I., Gordan, S., Ancient Logistics – Historical Timeline and etymology,Technical Gazette 18, EBSCO Host, June 2011, http://connection.ebscohost.com/c/ articles/67363071/ancient-logistics-historical-timeline-etymology, (accessed June 25, 2015).

2 . Oxford Dictionary On Line, Oxford University Press, 2015, http://www.oxforddictionaries. com/us, (accessed June 25, 2015).

3 . Tepic, J., Tanackov, I., Gordan, S., Ancient Logistics – Historical Timeline and etymology.

4. True Origin of Logistics & Supply Chain Revealed!, 2015, http://www.supplychainopz. com/2013/05/ logistics.html, (accessed June 25, 2015).

5. Godfrey, Major Frederick V., "The Logistics of Invasion", 2003, http://www.almc.army.mil/alog/issues/NovDec03/Logistics_of_Invasion.htm, (accessed June 25, 2015).

6. Major James J. McDonnell and Major J. Ronald Novack, "Logistics Challenges in Support of Operation Enduring Freedom", October 2004, http://www.alu.army.mil/alog/issues /SepOct04/freedom.html, (accessed July 20, 2015).

7. "Occupational Outlook Handbook: Logistics," Bureau of Labor Statistics, Department of Labor, January 8, 2014, http://www.bls.gov/ooh/business-and-financial/logisticians.htm#tab-1, (accessed June 25, 2015).

8. Smith, Jacquelyn, "The Happiest Jobs in America", Forbes.com, 2012, http://www.forbes.com/ sites/jacquelynsmith/2012/03/23/the-happiest-jobs-in-america, (accessed June 25, 2015).

9. "Order processor", Snagajob.com, 2015, http://www.snagajob.com/job-descriptions/order-entry-processor, (accessed June 30, 2015).

10 . "Trucking isn't a job or a career, it's a lifestyle: A truckers story", ABC News, 2013, http://abcnews.go.com/blogs/lifestyle/2013/11/trucking-isnt-a-job-or-a-career-its-a-lifestyle-a-truckers-story, (accessed June 30, 2015).

11. Combined Arms Support Command Public Affairs Office, "'Troops to Trucks' initiative kicks off at Fort Lee", Army.com, 2015, http://www.army.mil/article/79846/_Troops_to_Trucks__initiative_kicks_off_at_Fort_Lee, (accessed June 30, 2015).

12 . "Interview with an Auto Mechanic", Job Shadow, 2015, http://www.jobshadow.com/interview-with-an-auto-mechanic, (accessed June 30, 2015).

13. "How To Find The Right Training For A Career As A Mechanic", Truck Drivers Salary, 2015, http://truckdriversalary.net/mechanic-school, (accessed June 30, 2015).

14. "Fleet Maintenance Manager", Career Builder, 2015, http://www.careerbuilder.com/jobseeker/jobs, (accessed May 30, 2015).

15. "Operations and Supply Chain Management Career Paths and Patterns, Employment trends and professional paths you can put to work, A report produced by APICS The Association for Operations Management," APICS, 2014, http://www.apics.org/docs/cepd/operations-and-supply-chain-management-career-paths-and-patterns.pdf, (accessed June 30, 2015).

16. Andrea Carter, "5 ways to make your supply chain logistics career journey a smoother climb", Supply Chain 24/7, November 24, 2013, http://www.supplychain247.com/article/5_ways_to_make_your_supply_ chain_logistics_career_journey_a_smoother_climb, (accessed June 30, 2015).

17. "If You are in Supply Chain, You Made a Smart Career Choice", Supply Chain Digest, June 12, 2013, http://www.scdigest.com/ASSETS/ON_TARGET/13-06-12-1.php?cid=7128, (accessed June 30, 2015).

18. Melissa Korn, "The Hot New M.B.A.: Supply-Chain Management", The Wall Street Journal, June 2013, http://www.wsj.com/articles/SB10001424127887324423904578523591792789054, (accessed June 30, 2015).

19. Pirelli, "Supply Chain – Career Paths", June 2012, http://www.pirelli.com/corporate/en/careers/ career-paths/tyres/supply-chain/default.html, (accessed June 30, 2015).

20. Pirelli, "Supply Chain – Career Paths".

21. Pirelli, "Supply Chain – Career Paths".

22. "Operations and Supply Chain Management Career Paths and Patterns, Employment trends and professional paths you can put to work, A report produced by APICS The Association for Operations Management," APICS.

23. "Defense Acquisition Workforce Improvement Act (DAWIA)", Defense Acquisition University, December 18, 2013, http://www.dau.mil/doddacm/Pages/Certification.aspx, (accessed 6/22/2014).

24. "Certification & Core Plus Development Guides", Defense Acquisition University, December 18, 2013, http://icatalog.dau.mil/onlinecatalog/CareerLvl.aspx, (accessed 6/22/2014).

25. "Army e-Learning Program", Army.Com, 2015, http://www.armyreal.com/resources/item/890, (accessed June 30, 2015).

Chapter 4

1. Tranette Ledford, "The Best Jobs: Government Employee or Government Contractor?," ClearanceJobs, July 25, 2010, http://news.clearancejobs.com/2010/07/25/the-best-jobs-government-employee-or-government-contractor (accessed February 18, 2015).

2. Tranette Ledford, "The Best Jobs: Government Employee or Government Contractor?"

3. Tranette Ledford, "The Best Jobs: Government Employee or Government Contractor?"

4. "The Best Places to Work in the Federal Government 2013 Rankings," Partnership for Public Service, June 14, 2013, http://bestplacestowork.org/BPTW/rankings/governmentwide (accessed February 18, 2015).

5. "Benefits, Leave, and Pay for Federal Employees," USA.Gov, February 02, 2015, http://www.usa.gov/Federal-Employees/Benefits.shtml (accessed February 18, 2015).

6. Adam Stone, "Breaking down pros & cons of public & private sectors," Navy Times, March 26, 2014, http://www.navytimes.com/article/20140326/JOBS/303260044/Breaking -down-pros-cons-public-private-sectors/ (accessed February 18, 2015).

7. John Cibinic, Jr. and Ralph C. Nash, Jr., Administration of Government Contracts, Third Edition, (The George Washington University, Government Contracts Program, National Law Center, Washington D.C., 1995), 3.

8. Tranette Ledford, "The Best Jobs: Government Employee or Government Contractor?"

9. Adam Stone, "Breaking down pros & cons of public & private sectors," Navy Times, March 26, 2014, http://www.navytimes.com/ article/20140326/JOBS/303260044/Breaking-down-pros-cons-public-private-sectors/ (accessed February 18, 2015).

10. 401(k) Plans," Internal Revenue Service, October 14, 2014, http://www.irs.gov/Retirement-Plans/401(k)-Plans (accessed February 18, 2015).

11. The Consultants' Corner, "The Stark difference between private and public sector ERP implementations, Panorama Consulting Solutions, September 13, 2013, http://panorama-consulting.com/the-stark-difference-between-private-and-public-sector-erp-implementations/ (accessed February 18, 2015).

12. "Report of the Federal Salary Council Working Group," GovernmentExecutive.com, September, 2014, http://www.govexec.com/ media/gbc/docs/pdfs_edit/101714kl2.pdf (accessed February 18, 2015).

13. PRG Research Group, "Logistics Management's 30th Annual Salary Survey Results", March 04, 2014, http://www.supplychain247.com/ paper/logistics_managements_30th_annual_salary_ survey_results, (accessed June 30, 2015).

14. Richard Morgan, "Five Mandatory Benefits for Full-Time Employees," Houston Chronicle, http://smallbusiness.chron.com/five-mandatory-benefits-fulltime-employees-18874.html (accessed February 18, 2015).

15. "PricewaterhouseCoopers, LLP," Great Place to Work® Institute, November 11, 2014, http://us.greatrated.com/pwc/great-perks (accessed February 18, 2015).

16. "The Best Places to Work in the Federal Government 2013 Rankings."